CRICKET

PLAY THE GAME

CRICKET

IAN MORRISON

BLANDFORD

First published in Great Britain in 1989 by Ward
Lock Limited, Villiers House, 41–47 Strand,
London WC2N 5JE.
A Cassell Imprint

Reprinted 1990. This new edition published by
Blandford, 1993.
Reprinted 1993, 1994

Designed by Anita Ruddell
Figure drawings by Jerry Malone

Text set in Helvetica
by Hourds Typographica, Stafford, England
Printed in England by The Bath Press, Avon

British Library Cataloguing in Publication Data

Morrison, Ian *1947–*
    Cricket. (Play the game).
    1. Cricket
    I. Title   II. Series
    796.35′8

ISBN 0 7137 2409 9

Acknowledgments

The author and publishers would like to
thank Colorsport for supplying the
photographs reproduced in this book.

**Frontispiece: one of the game's great
characters and all-rounders, Ian Botham,
an expert with the bat, ball and at fielding.**

CONTENTS

FOREWORD

International cricket supremacy may swing every so often from one nation to another, but there is no doubting the pedigree of the game in England. The game's spread started on these shores and over the years we have produced some of the finest cricketers in the world; W. G. Grace, Herbert Sutcliffe, Wilfred Rhodes, Sir Leonard Hutton and more recently the likes of David Gower and Ian Botham.

Naturally, one must also recognize the role played by the great West Indians, Australians, New Zealanders, Indians and Pakistanis as the game has spread to all corners of the world.

Play the Game: Cricket offers an excellent starting point to any cricket fan who intends taking up the game, either leisurely or competitively, or is just content to watch the game from the armchair.

You will be treated to a fascinating historical look back to the eighteenth century when teams like Hambledon dominated the game, through to its present day and a similar domination by the West Indians in the 1970s and 80s.

To help you understand how cricket is played – and there are plenty of intricacies in this great game – the Game Guide takes you through the rules. The comprehensive Terminology section explains to you what terms like leg cutter, Chinaman, and googly all mean.

Rules to all games have those points which are open to interpretation or are not to clear to understand. The excellent Rules Clinic pinpoints, and answers, those argumentative points that may crop up during a game.

For those of you who want to go out and play the game, the technique section is particularly useful and will help you understand the basic principles of the game, whether it be as a batsman, bowler, or wicketkeeper.

The book, and indeed the whole series, has been designed around simplicity. We do not want to 'bog you down' with too many technicalities at an early stage of your cricketing development. *Play the Game* explains the basics, the rest is up to you. Reading a book will help, but to get any real benefit you must go out and play the game. And more important, you must practise.

Play the Game: Cricket will not turn you into a test cricketer, but it will set you on that road if you have such ambitions . . . the rest is down to you.

Ian Morrison

HISTORY & DEVELOPMENT OF CRICKET

Like many of the sports in the Ward Lock *Play the Game* series, cricket is another whose precise origins are not known. Cricket historians have been trying to trace the roots of England's national summer game for many years, but there is still uncertainty as to when exactly the game was born.

The first definite reference to cricket was in 1478 when a game called *criquet* was played at St Omer in north-east France. It is not until 1598 that reference to the sport was made in England. It came out in a court case involving a piece of land at Guildford in Surrey. During a dispute over the ownership of the land, John Derrick, a witness for one of the claimants, maintained he had played *krickett* on the land as a youngster. But Derrick did not elaborate on what form this game took. Unfortunately for the cricket historians, the judge was only interested in evidence relating to the ownership of the land, not how *krickett* was played.

The first cricket match on record took place in 1646, when two teams did battle at Coxheath in Kent, a town famous in more recent years for the Coxheath Men, world custard-pie throwing champions.

However, cricket, like many popular pastimes of the day, became subject to various edicts from the realm. In the most severe of these Oliver Cromwell ordered that all *krickett* sticks and balls should be burnt by the common hangman.

The first match between two English counties was played at Dartford Brent in 1709 when Kent and Surrey began a rivalry which has lasted 280 years. As the game spread, particularly in the Home Counties and the universities, there was a need to draw up some rules, and in 1744 the first Laws of Cricket were formulated by the London Club, of which Frederick Louis, Prince of Wales, was president.

Cricket attracted a lot of betting in its early days and the laws were designed as much to clarify rulings for gambling purposes as to resolve arguments between batsman and bowler.

Kent showed an early dominance as the game became very popular in the south of England, but in the latter half of the eighteenth century English cricket focused on a small Hampshire village ten miles north of Portsmouth. That village was Hambledon. Despite its size, the small community, thanks

CRICKET

to the efforts of Richard Nyren, landlord of the Bat & Ball Inn, mustered up great enthusiasm and support for the game of cricket. They played their matches at Broadhalfpenny Down, and soon attracted the best players in the area. Hambledon became the best team in the land and beat the challenges offered by the best county sides of the day. In 1777 they beat a fully represented England side by an innings and 168 runs at the Vine ground, Sevenoaks. This gives an indication of just how dominant Hambledon was at the time.

One of Hambledon's star batsmen of the day was John Small. Against Surrey at Broadhalfpenny Down in 1775 he scored 135; this is the first instance of a century on record.

The Hambledon supremacy lasted thirty-five years and only ended when their mentor Nyren moved to London in 1791.

During the Hampshire side's reign as 'champions', moves were being made in London to get the sport properly organized. The White Conduit Club was formed, playing their matches at White Conduit Fields in Islington. This club was to be the forerunner of the world-famous Marylebone Cricket Club, the MCC.

One member of the White Conduit was Yorkshireman Thomas Lord. Not a great cricketer, Lord was, however, a shrewd businessman. When the White Conduit's ground was threatened with closure to make way for building projects, Lord was instructed to find new premises on behalf of the club. He found and developed a new ground at what is now Dorset Square, near Marylebone Station, in 1787. Middlesex entertained Essex in the opening match at the first Lord's ground. That same year the White Conduit Club was dissolved and re-formed as the MCC. One of the MCC's first tasks was to revise the laws of the game. Since then the rules have undergone major revision only four times; in 1835, 1844, 1947 and 1980. The MCC was responsible for the government of all cricket from its formation in 1787 until 1969.

With the expiry of the lease on the Dorset Square ground in 1810, Thomas Lord was asked to find a new site for the MCC's ground. He dug up all the turves and transferred them three-quarters of a mile away to 'North Bank'. Within three years he was off again, after Parliament decreed that the new Regent's Canal should pass through the ground. Once more he transplanted the original turves. This time the move took Lord and the club to a site a few hundred yards to the north-west of the 'North Bank' site, and in 1814 the third Lord's ground was opened. This is the present home of the MCC and Middlesex County Cricket Club, and it still bears the name of the man who found and developed it, Thomas Lord. It is not, as many people incorrectly believe, so named because of some connection with the aristocracy.

By the mid-nineteenth century cricket's popularity had spread rapidly, but mostly in the southern half of England. Hambledon's successors as the new 'kings' of cricket were the All England XI, managed by George Parr. They used to play challenge matches against the county sides. One of the future stars of the All-England team was born in 1848. That man was to become a cricketing legend. His name? William Gilbert 'W.G.' Grace.

A giant of a man in both stature and ability, Grace brought a new element of skill to the game the likes of which had never been seen before. Extrovert, often to the point of eccentricity, he was the game's most outstanding all-rounder, as he set cricketing records and standards for all who followed him to beat.

Born in Downend, Bristol, Grace helped turn his native Gloucestershire into one of the leading first-class counties.

Wasim Akram has formed a successful partnership with Waqar Younis which has brought international wins for Pakistan.

CRICKET

By the time Grace made his first appearance in senior cricket at the age of sixteen, the game had grown in stature as one of England's most popular sports alongside horse racing. Matches between counties were becoming more regular, and more organized. Although an official championship did not exist, reference was made in 1853 to Nottinghamshire being the 'Champion County'.

People wanted to read about cricket as well as play and watch it. Publications sprang up; the press gave the sport extensive coverage and included comprehensive scorecards, and to fill the obvious demand for public enthusiasm John Wisden produced the first of his now famous almanacs in 1864.

As the county sides started to become properly constituted in the nineteenth century, it was inevitable an organized competition would not be far away. In 1864, with such counties as Kent, Hampshire, Lancashire, Middlesex, Nottinghamshire, Surrey, Sussex, Yorkshire and Cambridgeshire all being properly constituted, the first 'County Championship' took place – after a fashion. There were no strict rules of competition. Men could play for more than one county, the number of games a team played was not determined, and quite often the weaker teams shied away from matches against the stronger teams. The method of deciding the 'champion county' at the end of the season was left to the sporting newspapers of the day, but often they disagreed. However, Surrey were proclaimed the first 'champions' in 1864, albeit unofficially.

It was Nottinghamshire though, who became the great side of the era. Between 1865 and 1889 they won the 'title' 13 times. The northern teams had started to dominate the game for the first time, mainly because of their introduction of professionalism, while their southern counterparts remained amateur.

By 1873 the championship was no longer a casual affair, and certain rules existed, but, as only thirty-one matches constituted an entire season, the County Championship was a long way short of being what it is today. With the standard of play rising, and popularity amongst spectators increasing, there was a need to bring more uniformity and interest into the championship, and in 1890 it was reformed, with a points system being officially introduced for the first time. At last it was beginning to look like the Championship we now know. In 1895 the number of competing counties was increased to 14 and the Championship was, for the first time, truly representative of the first-class counties of the day and Surrey were crowned champions for the fifth time since the 1890 changes.

Worcestershire were admitted to the Championship in 1899, Northants in 1905 and Glamorgan in 1921. That makes up the total of seventeen first-class counties which existed until 1992 when the county of Durham was admitted.

By the end of the nineteenth century cricket had spread from its English roots and was being played in many overseas countries, notably those with British Empire connections.

English teams have been touring abroad since 1859, and that year the first expedition took an All-England XI, under the captaincy of George Parr, to Canada and the United States. That was the start of international cricket, forming the basis of present-day tours.

Cricket was not new to North America. A Mr William Byrd of Westover, Virginia is recorded as 'playing cricket with friends' in 1709, and in 1742 Highland Scots in Savannah, Georgia, USA, celebrated St Andrew's Day by playing cricket. (What an unlikely combination; a team of Scots playing cricket in the United States!)

In 1844 Canada and the United States played each other in an international match, making this the oldest fixture between two national sides in cricket; taking place thirty-three years before test cricket began.

Cricket was known to have been played on the continent of Europe in the mid-eighteenth century, and in 1721 mariners of the East India Company's ships played cricket at Cambay, in India. The other traditional test-playing nations also started to develop the game in the early part of the nineteenth century.

International cricket in the form of test matches started in 1877, when Australia and England took to the field at the Melbourne Cricket Ground on 15 March. Since then, South Africa in 1889, West Indies in 1928, New Zealand in 1930, India in 1932, Pakistan in 1952 and Sri Lanka in 1982, have all entered the test cricket arena. South Africa, after more than 30 years of exclusion, now look likely to regain its permanent international status.

Because of the amount of cricket being played worldwide, and at varying levels, there was a need to distinguish between the various types of cricket. Certain matches were designated as being first-class from 1815, but over the years the definition and identification of matches as being first-class has posed problems to the game's historians and statisticians. However, in 1947 the term was defined officially for the first time.

The one form of the game that is not included as 'first-class' is the limited overs game, so called because it is not spread over a number of days like county or test cricket, but must be completed in a limited number of overs bowled by each side.

The first limited overs competition was the Gillette Cup (now the National Westminster Bank Trophy) which was first contested in 1963. It is still the sport's leading one-day game in England and culminates with the final being played at Lord's at the end of the season. The John Player Sunday League (now the Refuge Assurance League), followed in 1969 and is a season-long competition involving all the first-class counties, who play each other once. From 1988 the top four teams played off for the title at the end of the season. All matches except the play-offs are played on a Sunday.

The third and final limited overs competition for the major sides was launched in 1972, when Benson & Hedges announced their new competition. It is initially a round-robin competition with the leading eight teams progressing to a knockout stage. The final is played at Lord's during the season.

Inevitably, with the introduction of limited overs cricket into the domestic game, it followed that the same would happen in the international game. On 5 January 1971 Australia beat England by five wickets in the first One Day International at Melbourne. Since then numerous one day international contests have been introduced and nearly all touring sides play a series of one day internationals alongside their test commitments. Cricket's World Cup was launched in England in 1975 and is played every four years.

Floodlit limited over cricket was introduced in the late 1970s as part of the Kerry Packer 'Circus' and became popular in Australia.

The limited over game is the biggest innovation to hit cricket since the birth of the county championship and is destined to see dramatic changes in the coming years. But what else has happened to the game? Well, there have been modifications to the format of the championship over the years, with the introduction of bonus points and standardizing the number of games played. The number of balls per over has been experimented with; on occasion it has been increased from six to eight, and decreased from six to four.

The game has certainly been privileged to witness some of the giants of the sporting world grace its playing arenas. There have been top batsmen such as Jack Hobbs, Walter Hammond, Denis Compton and Len Hutton. Bowlers Wilf Rhodes, 'Titch' Freeman, Jim Laker and Dennis Lillee. Wicketkeepers like Bob Taylor, Godfrey Evans, Rodney Marsh and Alan Knott. All-rounders like Gary Sobers, Kapil Dev and

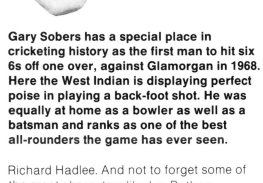

Gary Sobers has a special place in cricketing history as the first man to hit six 6s off one over, against Glamorgan in 1968. Here the West Indian is displaying perfect poise in playing a back-foot shot. He was equally at home as a bowler as well as a batsman and ranks as one of the best all-rounders the game has ever seen.

Richard Hadlee. And not to forget some of the great characters like Ian Botham, Freddie Trueman and, of course, the legendary W.G. Grace.

Naturally, cricket equipment has seen some changes. Cricket can now be played indoors on artificial surfaces, and, indeed, it can be played *outdoors* on artificial surfaces. A far cry from the pioneering days at Broadhalfpenny Down!

The artificial pitch is just one of the many advances and changes over the years. The cricket bat, for example, has also come a long way. It now has maximum dimensions of $4\frac{1}{4}$ in (10.8cm) wide and 38in (96.5cm) long. Early bats however, were very different. They were not flat-faced, but rounded, looking a bit like a hockey stick . . . great for scooping a ball over the slips, but not too good for directing a drive over the bowler's head!

Whilst the pitch has always been around its present-day 22yd (20.12m) length, the stumps, however, have seen many changes over the years. In the early seventeenth century they were up to 6ft (1.83m) wide and less than 12in (30.48cm) tall in some cases. By the end of the century they had been reduced to 2ft (60.96cm) and 1ft (30.48cm) high. The third stump was not introduced until around 1775, when members of the Hambledon club used it in one of their matches. It became compulsory ten years later.

By 1775 the wicket was only 6in (15.24cm) wide and 22in (55.88cm) high. It underwent a further change towards the end of the eighteenth century: this time it was 2ft (60.96cm) tall and 7in (17.78cm) wide. It became 26in (66.04cm) tall in 1819 and in 1823 it measured 27in (68.58cm) tall and 8in (20.32cm) wide. That was it for over 100 years, until 1931 to be exact, when the present-day dimensions of 28in (71.1cm) by 9in (22.86cm) were introduced. Early stumps only had one bail. The two bails are believed to have been introduced around 1785.

Cricket fashions have also changed over the years. Players in the early eighteenth century used to play in three-cornered or jockey hats, covered in silver or gold lace. They wore breeches, silk stockings and buckled shoes. There were none of the white casual sweaters in those days; players had to wear buttoned coats.

In the first half of the nineteenth century trousers started to replace breeches. Hats were still worn, but more of the tall 'beaver' style. High-collared shirts were also the vogue. In the second half of the century the tall hat gave way to the peaked cap. And, following the lead of the I Zingari Club, other clubs started introducing their own colours, now very much part of cricketing tradition. The now traditional all-white started to appear towards the end of the nineteenth century as the cricketer started to look like the man we know today. Sorry! delete man and insert 'person', because women cricketers must not be forgotten. After all, they have been playing the game since 1745, when the first ladies' match on record took place at Gosden Common in Surrey.

Although not organized on such a large scale as the men's game, women's cricket is nevertheless played with the same enthusiasm and relative level of skill. England and Australia provide the backbone of international ladies' cricket and the two nations have been doing battle since their first test encounter at Brisbane in December 1934.

All cricket, whether it be the first-class game, the club game, or the women's game, depends on its grass-roots level, and the schools play a large part in developing future talent. Youngsters who show that bit of extra-special talent are encouraged to attend one of the many cricketing schools that exist around the country.

The National Cricket Association employs top-class coaches who want to see the game bettered and developed nationwide. The Association would willingly offer advice to any budding youngster who thinks he may have a future in the game.

Some youngsters go on to make the grade in the first-class game, but for every one who does, there are hundreds who do not. Happily the structure of cricket in Britain, thanks to the many local leagues, offers plenty of opportunities for you to play cricket in your area.

Cricket is a great game, not only for its participancy on the field but for its social atmosphere. It is a game which involves all members of the family, and the good, clean-cut image of the sport has not been tarnished over the years, unlike some sports. Another plus in cricket's favour is that age is no barrier. Youngsters and old alike may be seen competing together all over the country every weekend during the summer.

Cricket is both a terrific game to watch and a terrific game to play. With *Play the Game; Cricket* you will get that something extra out of the game, either as a spectator, or as a player. We do not expect to be able to turn you into an Ian Botham or Waqar Younis, but we can help you to understand the game to its fullest. The rest is up to you. Put into it what you want out of it and you will get years of pleasure from the greatest of all summer games.

EQUIPMENT & TERMINOLOGY

Cricket is a bat and ball team game played by eleven players per side. Play takes place on a large grassed area with a pitch cut in a position near the centre of the field. The pitch is a flat, rolled and finely cut area on which the battle between bowler and batsman takes place. Synthetic pitches are occasionally used, but they are not as satisfactory as natural, carefully manicured, surfaces.

Apart from the bat and ball the only other equipment essential to get a game of cricket started is a set of wickets; three wooden stumps, and two wooden bails. With that basic equipment, and a few players, a game of cricket can be got under way. Mind you, stumps are not always essential: street games are often played with three 'stumps' being chalked on a wall, or a nearby lamp post or tree can serve just as well. If you are playing in the street, beware – broken windows cost a fair chunk of the weekly pocket money . . .

Because cricket is played with a hard ball, batsmen and fielders wear protection against injury. The batsman wears pads on his legs, padded gloves and occasionally a reinforced helmet. Some batsmen also like to wear protective arm and/or thigh pads.

Wicketkeepers are also protected with leg pads and wear larger gloves. Occasionally outfielders who field in a position close to the wicket wear protective helmets. All players should wear a 'box', a protective fibre glass moulded cover for those 'delicate' parts of the body . . . this does not apply to women!

Let us have a closer look at cricketing equipment.

The playing field

Strangely, the rules of the game do not stipulate the overall size of the playing field. The laws do, however, stipulate that the extremity of the playing field should be marked in some way to indicate the perimeter of the boundary. The markings can take the form of a rope, white marking, or some similar form. The boundary is not marked from any specific point and local conditions and overall size of the playing area dictate the position of the boundary fence.

The Pitch

The laws, however, do stipulate the size of the pitch; the area between the two bowling creases (see opposite). At each end of the pitch are positioned three stumps which are placed 22yd (20.12m) apart. The width of the pitch is 10ft (3.04m) with the centre being on a line drawn between the two middle stumps.

Most grounds have more than one pitch cut and ready for use. However, once play

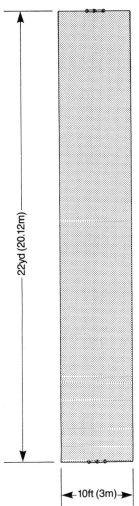

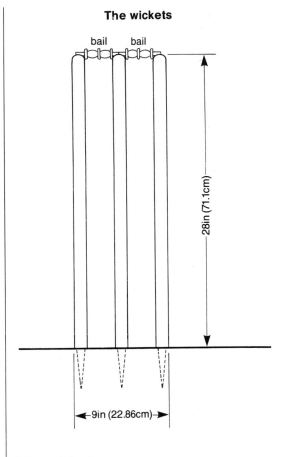

The wickets

The pitch

The pitch and its dimensions. It is cut and prepared and is positioned somewhere near the centre of the playing field.

has started on one pitch, it cannot be transferred to another unless in exceptional circumstances.

If the playing surface is artificial, or non-turf, then its minimum length should be 58ft (17.68m) and at least 6ft (1.83m) wide, although the distance between the stumps should still be 22yd (20.12m).

The wickets

A set of wickets consists of three equally-sized wooden stumps and two wooden bails. Two sets are positioned on the pitch 22yd (20.12m) apart and opposite and parallel to each other.

Each stump is 28in (71.1cm) in height from the ground to the top of the stump. The actual length is about 31–32in (78.74–81.28cm), but only 28in (71.1cm) is above ground. The total width of the three stumps is 9in (22.86cm) and they should be positioned in a straight line and equally spaced so as to prevent the ball passing between any two stumps. The tops of the stumps are dome-shaped with grooves cut to accommodate the bails.

CRICKET

The bails are $4\frac{3}{8}$in (11.1cm) long and when in position should not protrude more than $\frac{1}{2}$in (1.3cm) above the top of the stump.

In junior cricket the sizes of the wickets are slightly smaller, as follows:

- (a) width: 8in (20.32cm)
- (b) distance apart: 21yd (19.20m)
- (c) Height: 27in (68.58cm)
- (d) Bails: $3\frac{7}{8}$in (9.84cm) long (each)

The creases

At each end of the pitch are marked creases. These are areas which dictate where the bowler may place his feet when delivering. They also indicate the area in which the batsman must stand, and that which he must reach when making a run. This is known as his 'ground'. There are three creases (a) the bowling crease (b) the popping crease and (c) the return crease.

The **bowling crease** is the line along which the stumps are pitched. The length of the crease is 8ft 8in (2.64m) and the stumps shall be pitched in the middle of the line.

The **popping crease** is marked parallel to the bowling crease and in front of the wickets. The distance from the middle of the wicket to the near edge of the popping crease is 4ft (1.22m). The length of the popping crease shall be a minimum of 6ft (1.83m) on either side of the line of the wicket. Although not so marked, its length is

The creases

The creases

considered to be unlimited for the purpose of the laws of the game.

The **return crease** is drawn at right angles from each end of the bowling crease and joins the popping crease and extends behind the wicket the other way. It must be marked a minimum of 4ft (1.22m) behind the wicket and is assumed to be unlimited in length for the purpose of the laws of the game.

The bat

Despite attempts to get around the rules by playing with an aluminium bat a few years ago, Australian test player Dennis Lillee soon found it outlawed. The laws of the game clearly state the blade of the bat must be made of wood. The blade can, however, be covered in a protective material provided it does not exceed ⅟₁₆in (1.56mm) in thickness.

The overall length of the bat must not exceed 38in (96.5cm) and the blade should not exceed $4\frac{1}{4}$in (10.8cm) at its widest part.

Bats are made out of willow (either English willow or the cheaper Kashmir willow) and come in a variety of sizes (subject to the maximum), and weights, which vary, generally between 2lb 6oz and 3lb (1.08–1.36kg).

A young person selecting a bat for the first time would do well to choose one that is not too heavy. Pick the bat up with the top hand only – how it feels to you (not whether it is endorsed by your favourite player) is most important.

When you buy a bat there will most likely be a plastic film over the blade. However, if the bat is pure willow, you need to lightly oil the face before you first use it, but be careful not to oil the splice (the part where the handle joins the blade).

Before using a new bat in a match it is best to knock up a few times using an old ball, or strike the blade with a special bat mallet.

A few useful tips; look down the grain of

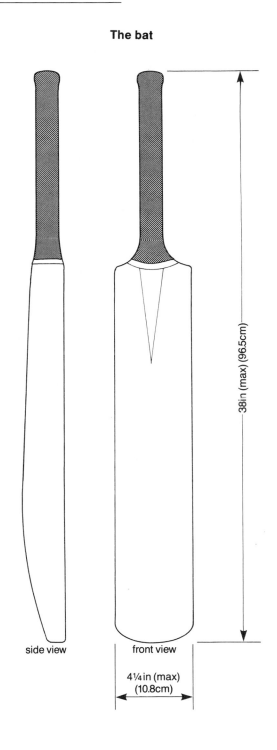

The bat

side view   front view

38in (max) (96.5cm)

4¼in (max) (10.8cm)

the blade, make sure the grain is straight and not too wide, or too narrow, and make sure there are no knots in it. Look closely at the manufacture of the handle, this is important. A good handle is made out of thin strips of cane which are planed and stuck together and assembled with rubber strips extending the full length of the handle. Cheaper bats have handles with rubber strips that do not go the full length. Watch out for this.

The handle is covered in a rubber casing for an easier grip. The majority of bats are produced with short handles, however, if you are tall you will most probably want a longer-handled bat. Most good sports goods shops stock an extensive range of bats. Take your time trying them out before you choose the one you want.

The ball

The ball is round and cased in stitched red leather. The weight shall be between $5\frac{1}{2}$–$5\frac{3}{4}$oz (155.9–163g) and its circumference between $8\frac{13}{16}$–9 in (22.4–22.9cm).

These dimensions apply to the ball used in the senior game. The laws permit tolerances for other standards of play, as follows:

Men's Grade 2–4:
Weight: $5\frac{5}{16}$–$5\frac{13}{16}$oz (150–165g)
Circumference: $8\frac{11}{16}$–$9\frac{1}{16}$in (22–23cm)

Women:
Weight: $4\frac{15}{16}$–$5\frac{5}{16}$oz (140–150g)
Circumference: $8\frac{1}{4}$–$8\frac{7}{8}$in (21–22.5cm)

Junior:
Weight: $4\frac{5}{16}$–$5\frac{1}{16}$oz (133–143g)
Circumference: $8\frac{1}{16}$–$8\frac{11}{16}$in (20.5–22cm)

In the middle of top quality balls there is a cork cube, around which are wound alternate layers of cork and wool until a sphere of the correct size is formed. This is then covered with finest leather and a continuous seam is stitched around the outside. The seam plays an important part in the bowler's delivery, as you will see in the technique section later on.

Clothing

Players traditionally wear all-white trousers, white shoes, white shirts and white jumpers – the latter often with their club/county colours as a trim. In matches played under floodlights, however, players wear pastel-coloured outfits.

All players wear special **shoes** which are generally made of leather and have spiked soles. Some modern shoes, however, are made with full dimpled rubber soles. Shoes used to be large and rather cumbersome like boots, but many modern-day shoes resemble a modern football boot, cut away at the ankle and very lightweight. Top-class players wear different shoes depending on whether they are batting, fielding or bowling.

Protective leg **pads** are made of either canvas or buckskin outers over cane and sidewing padding. Most pads have either two or three vertical foam-filled bolsters for

The ball

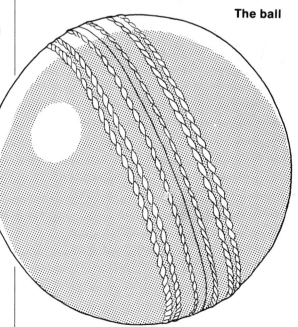

added protection around the knee area. Three straps enable the pads to be buckled at the back of the leg. Pads come in varying sizes and it is important to make sure you feel comfortable. Wicket-keeping pads tend to be shorter than batting pads and finish just above the knee. They do, however, still provide ample protection, and give freedom of movement.

When you first put a set of pads on they will feel uncomfortable and strange. But it won't take long for you to get used to them. You must wear them as protection against the ball whether it be as a batsman or wicketkeeper.

Protective **gloves** are also essential for both the batsman and wicketkeeper. The batting gloves have a leather palm to ensure a good grip on the bat. The back of the glove is covered with foam-filled protectors in the shape of pre-bent fingers. Wicket keeping gloves are totally different. They are made of leather and are leather-lined, with cane and sponge protection built into them.

Thigh and arm pads are canvas over a polystyrene pad protector.

Protective helmets, as worn by batsmen and close infielders, are metal or fibre-glass and can have a chin strap, ear protectors, and nose guard according to personal choice . . . and the pace of the opposing bowler!

If you buy your own equipment you will need something strong to carry it all around in, so it is worth investing in a good quality canvas or leather bag. Don't forget to put a few obvious items in the bag like a towel and talcum powder because cricket can become hot work . . .

Items of equipment to be found elsewhere on the cricket field include the sightscreen, scoreboard, and covers.

There should be two **sightscreens**, one on the boundary fence behind each set of wickets. They are large white areas (often wooden) measuring anything from as little as 20ft (6.10m) wide and 15ft (4.57m) high. These are approximate dimensions. The

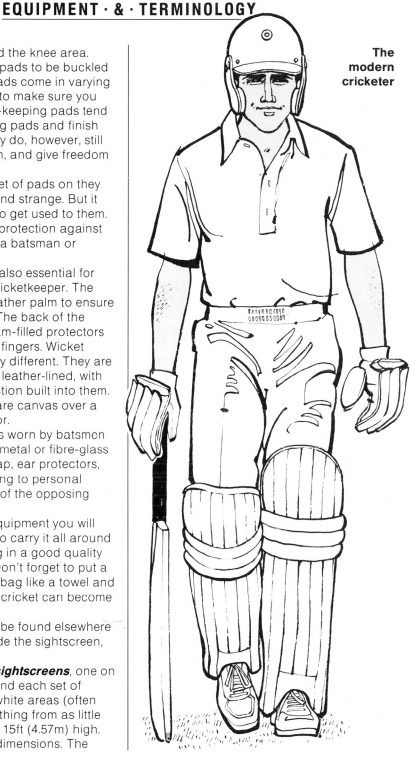

The modern cricketer

laws of the game do not state the sizes of sightscreens. Local conditions dictate their size.

The purpose of the sightscreens is to give the batsmen a clear sighting of the bowler's arm as he makes his delivery. Spectators should not walk or move in front of the sightscreens when a bowler is in action.

All cricket grounds have a **scoreboard**. Major grounds have large electronic boards which highlight most of the action on the field right down to the maiden name of the first slip's grandmother! At club level, however, scoreboards are basic and will advise only the current team total, number of wickets fallen, which batsmen are at the crease and how many runs each has made, and the score at the fall of the last wicket.

Cricket thrives on its statistical analysis, and all teams – whether they be the fourth eleven of the local village team or the England test team – have a scorer. He (or she; a lot of scorers are women), catalogues details of runs made (and not made), dismissals, bowling returns, fall of wickets and so on, thus enabling an analysis of individual batting and bowling performances in each match.

The larger cricket grounds have **covers** to protect the pitch during spells of rain. These are large movable items on wheels which can be easily wheeled into place at the first sign of rain, and give protection to the playing surface.

The last item of cricket equipment is the **roller**. The state of any pitch depends upon the quality of the work done with this tool by the groundsman. Most take great care and pride in their work and build up a close rapport with their roller. The pitch must be perfectly flat, and regular rolling is the only way to maintain it at its peak. A pitch can

Graeme Hick – the man of the year in 1988. This picture shows him dressed in typical attire of the modern-day batsman with the protective helmet and visor. All that is missing are the arm pads.

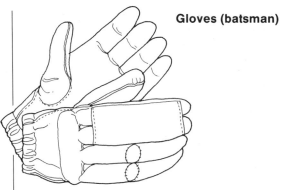

Gloves (batsman)

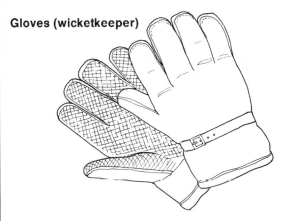

Gloves (wicketkeeper)

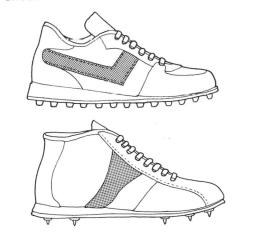

Shoes

Modern-day cricket shoes can either be low at the ankle, or with ankle protectors. Twenty years ago, all boots had ankle protectors.

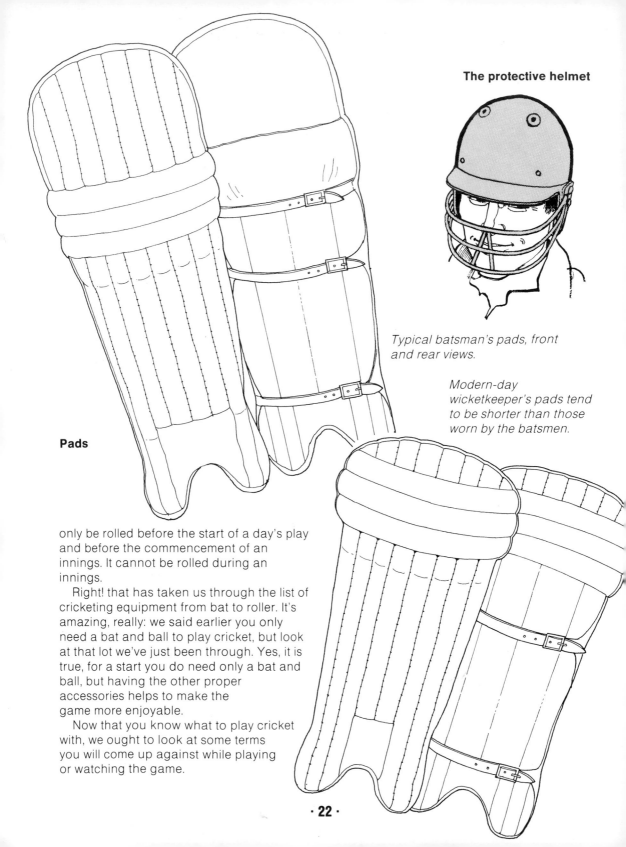

The protective helmet

Pads

Typical batsman's pads, front and rear views.

Modern-day wicketkeeper's pads tend to be shorter than those worn by the batsmen.

only be rolled before the start of a day's play and before the commencement of an innings. It cannot be rolled during an innings.

Right! that has taken us through the list of cricketing equipment from bat to roller. It's amazing, really: we said earlier you only need a bat and ball to play cricket, but look at that lot we've just been through. Yes, it is true, for a start you do need only a bat and ball, but having the other proper accessories helps to make the game more enjoyable.

Now that you know what to play cricket with, we ought to look at some terms you will come up against while playing or watching the game.

Sightscreen

A typical wooden sightscreen as found on many club grounds.

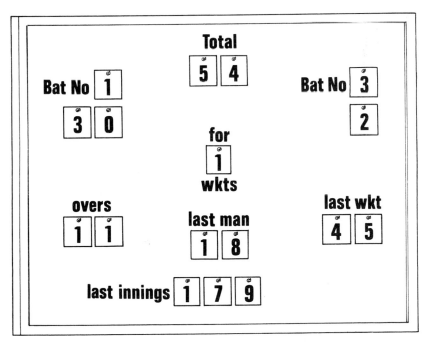

Scoreboard

A basic scoreboard which shows the home team having scored 54 for 1 in reply to the visitors' score of 179. Batsman No. 1 has scored 30, No. 3 has scored 2 and there have been 4 extras. The last man scored 18 and the last wicket fell at 45 runs. The match is in its 11th over. The figures are removable.

TERMINOLOGY

All rounder A good, competent player capable of batting, bowling and proving his worth as a fielder as well.

Appeal A loud call by a fielder, often the bowler, to an umpire to give the batsman out. A batsman cannot be given out unless an appeal is made to the umpire.

Backing up To prevent overthrows, one fielder will stand behind another at the wicket in readiness for any possible misfielding.

Batting average A player's batting average is calculated by dividing the number of runs scored by the number of innings played less the number of times he has been not out.

Block Mark made by the batsman with the toe of his bat in front of the wicket when taking guard. See also 'guard'. It is also the term used to describe a defensive shot made by a batsman with no intention of making a run.

Bouncer A fast delivery pitched short of a length which reaches the batsman at shoulder height . . . or above.

Bowled A batsman is bowled out if the ball hits his wicket and dislodges a bail. It does not matter if the ball hits the wicket direct or comes off his bat or person, he is still out bowled.

Bowling average A player's bowling average is calculated by dividing the number of runs conceded by the number of wickets taken.

Batting average

M	I	NO	RUNS	HS	AVGE	100	50
28	53	2	1167	155	22.88	2	4

This example shows a player's batting average of 22.88 runs per innings. This is how the figures generally appear in newspapers and magazines. In this example, the batsman has played in 28 matches and batted in 53 innings. He has been not out twice and scored a total of 1,167 runs. His highest score has been 155 not out and his average is calculated by dividing 1,167 by 51 (innings less not outs). He had made two centuries, and has four times made a score of 50 or more.

Bowling average

O	M	RUNS	WKTS	AVGE	BEST	5 WI	10 WM
166	12	313	11	28.45	5-55	1	0

This example shows a bowler's average of 28.45, i.e. one wicket is taken every 28.45 runs. The figures show he bowled 166 overs, of which 12 were maiden overs. He conceded 313 runs off his bowling and took 11 wickets at an average of 28.45. His best analysis in any one innings was 5 wickets for 55 runs and he has once claimed 5 victims in one innings but, as yet, has never taken 10 wickets in a match.

Break   A term used to describe the movement of the ball off a straight path on hitting the pitch.

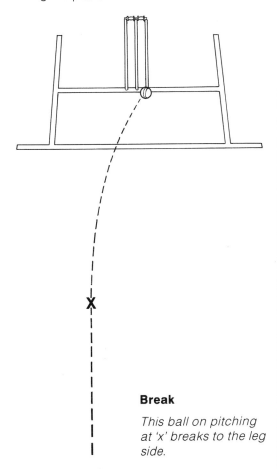

Break

This ball on pitching at 'x' breaks to the leg side.

Bump ball   A ball that hits the ground immediately after striking the bat before rising in the air. From the comfort of the stands it is often difficult to assess whether it is a bump ball or a catch.

Bye   Any run that is made when the ball passes the wicket untouched by the bat is a bye. If the ball is unintentionally deflected past the wicket by the batsman, other than by his hand holding the bat (or the bat itself), and runs are scored, these are called leg byes. Wides and no-balls are not byes.

Call   When one batsman shouts at the other to run.

Carry the bat   If one of the opening batsmen is still not out when all the other 10 batsmen have been dismissed, he is said to have carried his bat throughout the innings.

Caught   A batsman is out *caught* if the ball travels direct from his bat to a fielder's hands before hitting the ground.

Century   An individual score of 100.

Chinaman   An off-break delivery by a left-armed bowler to a right-handed batsman.

Close field   The fielders who take up positions close to the batsman are said to be the close field.

Cut   A stroke made at a short-pitched ball on the off side. The bat is held horizontally at the time of making the stroke.

Dead ball   There are many instances when the ball is deemed to be 'dead'. The main ones occur when:

(a) It has finally settled in the hands of the bowler or wicketkeeper.
(b) It reaches or lands over the boundary.
(c) A batsman is out.
(d) It lodges in the clothing of a batsman or umpire, or the protective headgear of a member of the fielding side.
(e) the umpire calls an end to an over, or the day's play.

The umpire can also call the ball 'dead' in other instances. For example: if a player has been seriously injured and requires attention, the bails fall off the stumps before a ball is delivered, or the bowler accidentally drops the ball.
   Once the bowler has started his run-up or bowling action, the ball is no longer 'dead'.

CRICKET

Declaration   A team may make a declaration at any time by declaring their innings closed. They do not have to wait for all the wickets to be dismissed. Declarations are made in an effort to produce a result rather than letting the match be drawn. Declarations are not allowed in senior limited over matches.

Deep   The part of the field away from the pitch and near to the boundary.

Delivery   A bowled ball is called a delivery.

Draw   Any match that fails to produce a result is a draw.

Drive   A stroke where power is exerted by the batsman as he strikes the ball foreward or sideways.

Duck   A score of nought (0). See also 'golden duck'.

Extras   All runs added to the score made other than with the bat are called extras. Byes, leg-byes, wides and no-balls are all extras, but the last two count against the bowler's analysis.

Flight   The path of the ball whilst in the air.

Follow-on   In a match of two innings per side, the team batting second can be asked to bat again if their first innings total falls short of the first team's innings by a certain amount. This amount varies according to the length of a match. If it is a five-day match then a team follows-on if they are 200 runs behind the first team's score. If a three-day game, then the follow-on is invited when the team batting second is 150 or more runs behind. The same applies when the second team is 100 runs behind in a two-day match and 75 runs behind if the match is of one day duration but over two innings.

Forward stroke   If the batsman advances his front foot down the wicket in order to play the ball as near as possible to where it pitches, he is said to be making a 'forward strike'.

Full toss   A ball delivered that reaches the batsman without hitting the ground first. Also known as a 'full pitch'.

Glance   A ball deflected off the face of the bat is a glance. It is often made down the leg-side.

Golden duck   When a player is dismissed on his first ball.

Googly   An off-break delivery made with a leg-break bowling action.

Guard   The batsman always like to know where his bat is in relation to the wicket. When he first comes to the wicket (and when he bats from the opposite end for the first time) he will ask the umpire to guide him to his preferred position – known as the 'guard'. The umpire will line up the position by looking down the pitch over the bowler's wickets. The batsman will request that his bat is lined up with, say, the middle stump, halfway between middle and leg, or the leg stump, and so on. Once lined up, the batsman will make his block.

Gully   A fielder who stands close in and between the slips and point.

Half volley   A delivery hit near to the front foot, and an instant after it has bounced.

Handled ball   A form of dismissal. Either batsman shall be given out if he deliberately touches the ball with his hands while it is still in play, unless with the consent of the opposing side.

Hat trick   A bowler performs the hat trick if he claims three victims with successive deliveries. They need not be in the same over – indeed, not even in the same innings – but must be in the same match to count.

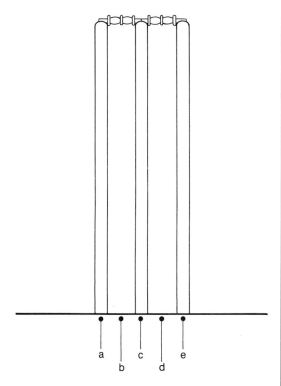

a   c   e
b   d

Guard

The guards a batsman will ask for:

(a) *OFF*
(b) *MIDDLE-AND-OFF*
(c) *MIDDLE*
(d) *MIDDLE-AND-LEG*
(e) *LEG*

(These apply to right-handed batsmen, they are the other way around for left-handers.)

Most batsmen will ask the umpire for a number:

1. *LEG STUMP*
2. *MIDDLE-AND-LEG*
3. *MIDDLE etc.*

Middle-and-Off and Off are rarely asked for because of the high risk of lbw. Sometimes for Middle-and-Leg a batsman will ask for 'Two'.

Hit the ball twice   Another form of dismissal. If a batsman hits the ball twice he is given out. A batsman can, however, hit the ball a second time in order to stop it hitting his wicket.

Hit wicket   A batman shall be out 'hit wicket' if he hits the wicket and dislodges a bail with any part of his person or equipment, including the bat, while preparing to receive, or whilst receiving a delivery. He is also out if he hits his wicket while setting off on his first run immediately after playing, or playing at, the ball.

Hook   A stroke made off the back foot at a delivery pitched short. Normally made just above waist height, it is hit to the leg-side.

Inswinger   A delivery that moves from the off to leg side whilst in flight.

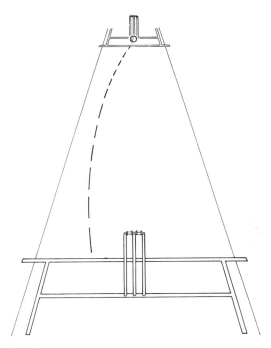

Inswinger

A ball that moves from off to leg in flight is an inswinger.

Leg before wicket This will be explained in greater detail in the 'Game Guide' and 'Rules Clinic' because it is one of the game's most complex areas. It is a form of dismissal whereby the ball pitches against the batman's body in a way which would otherwise have resulted in him being bowled. But it is not quite as simple as that. For a full explanation see page 37.

Leg break A ball that moves from leg to off after pitching.

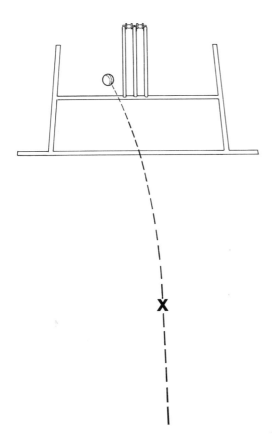

Leg break

A ball that moves from leg to off after pitching at 'x' is a leg break.

Leg bye See Bye.

Leg cutter A type of delivery. It is perfected by cutting the fingers across the seam. It is a fast leg-break.

Leg side The side of the field behind the batsman as he takes up his normal stance at the crease. Also known as the 'on side'.

Length All bowlers try to find a good *length* – the point where the ball pitches. A delivery with perfect length will be a difficult one for the batsman to play, often leaving him undecided what shot to attempt.

Long leg A fielding position near to the boundary, behind the wicket on the leg side.

Long off Another fielding position near to the boundary, but this time at the bowler's end of the field. The long off stands to the side of the sightscreen.

Long on He stands the other side of the sightscreen from the long off.

Long stop Although the senior game no longer uses a long stop, he can still be found in kids' games in the local park. He fields behind the wicketkeeper.

Maiden over An over in which the batsman fails to score a run off the bowling. See also wicket maiden.

Middle The name given to the area of the playing area where the pitch is prepared.

Night watchman When a side is put into bat towards the end of a day's play, a team will often put a low order batsman in to bat as a partner for a more experienced batsman, so as to preserve the better batsmen until the following day's play.

No-ball A delivery from a bowler that the umpire considers to be unfair is a 'no-ball'.

The bowler has an extra delivery at the end of the over to replace it. A batsman can score runs in the normal way off a no-ball and he can be dismissed, but not if he is bowled, caught, stumped or lbw.

Not out If a team's innings ends and a batsman has not been dismissed, he is said to be 'not out'.

Obstructing the field A batsman can be out for obstructing another player, either by action or words.

Off break A delivery that turns from off to leg after pitching.

Off Cutter A fast off-breaking delivery that is performed by 'cutting' the fingers across the seam of the ball at delivery.

Off drive A drive between cover and mid-off.

Off side The side of the field in front of the batsman when he takes up his stance at the crease.

On drive A drive, like most other drives, made from off the front foot. It is hit between mid-wicket and mid-on.

On side See Leg side.

Outfield The part of the playing area away from the pitch or surrounding area.

Outswinger A delivery that moves from leg to off while in flight is an outswinger.

Over the wicket A method of bowling in which the bowler delivers the ball with his bowling hand nearest to the stumps.

Over An over consists of either six or eight deliveries from the bowler from one end of the pitch. The number of balls per over are decided before the match or as governed by

Outswinger

A ball that moves from leg to off while in flight is an outswinger.

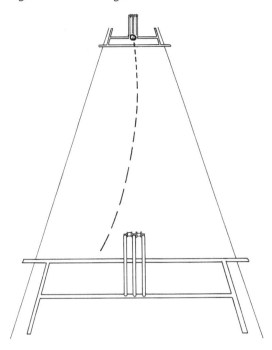

the rules of the competition. Overs are delivered from alternate ends of the pitch, and no bowler may bowl consecutive overs in one innings.

Overthrow A throw from a fielder that passes the wicketkeeper, or fielder at the stumps, and enables the runners to add more runs to their total.

Pair When a batsman is out for two ducks in one match he is said to have 'bagged a pair'. So called because two noughts resemble a *pair* of spectacles (0–0).

Played on When the batsman plays the ball on to his own wicket he is said to have played on and is given out. Playing on is classed as being bowled, and the bowler takes credit for the dismissal.

Point   A close-in fielding position square with the wicket on the off side.

Pull   A powerful stroke pulling the ball off the back foot and hit between mid-on and mid-wicket. It is normally effected when the ball is pitched outside the leg stump.

Return   The throw by a fielder to either wicket after fielding the ball.

Round the wicket   The opposite to 'over the wicket'. The bowler delivers the ball with the hand furthest away from the stumps.

Run(s)   Runs can be scored either by hitting the ball over the boundary, when, ironically, it is not necessary to run, or, as the name implies, by running between the wickets until it is felt it is no longer safe to carry on running. When running, the batsmen must each ground their bats over the two popping creases for the run to count. Runs can also be scored as a result of penalties being added, for no-balls, wides, etc.

Runner   If a batsman is prohibited from running due to injury or illness, another player from his own side is allowed to act as his runner. The runner should, preferably, have already batted, and to make it fair, must be fitted with the same external equipment as the batter for whom he is 'running'.

Run out   If a batsman is running between the two popping creases and a fielder hits the wicket and removes the bails with the ball before the batsman grounds his bat, then the batsman is 'run out'. If both batsmen are out of their ground then the one nearest the wicket that is 'put down' is out.

Seam bowler   A medium-paced bowler who utilizes the seam of the ball to cause it to deviate from its line once it pitches by getting it to pitch on the seam rather than using his fingers to effect spin.

Short leg   A close-in fielder on the leg side. He can be either forward short-leg, square short-leg, or backward short-leg, depending upon where he stands in relation to the batsman's wicket.

Short run   If the batsman fails to ground his bat behind the popping crease while making a run it is called a short run and not counted.

Single   A name for a single run.

Slip   A fielding position on the off side and close to the wicketkeeper. First slip stands next to the 'keeper. Second slip next to him, and so on.

Square cut   A stroke made off the back foot to a short delivery just outside the off stump. The ball is directed to just behind point.

Stumped   Another form of dismissal. If, after playing and missing the ball, the batsman is out of his ground, the wicketkeeper can 'break' the wicket by removing a bail either with the ball or with his gloved hand holding the ball. The batsman is also out stumped if the ball rebounds off the wicketkeeper onto the stumps, provided the batsman is out of his ground.

Substitute   See Twelfth man.

Sundries   The Australian term for 'extras'.

Sweep   A batting stroke made off the front foot with the back knee virtually on the ground. It is normally made to a ball pitched on or outside leg stump.

Tie   If the aggregate scores of both sides are level after all wickets have been lost, then the match is declared a tie. It is a rare occurrence in the first-class game and has happened only twice in test cricket.

Timed out A batsman is allowed two minutes from the moment the last wicket falls until the moment he steps on to the field of play. If he takes longer he can be dismissed 'timed out'.

Track Another name for the pitch.

Twelfth man Replacement fielders are allowed on to the field in place of injured or otherwise indisposed players. The twelfth man cannot, however, bat or bowl, and any catches he makes are credited to 'sub'.

Umpires The officials who show complete impartiality in enforcing the laws of the game. There are two umpires in every match, one officiating from the bowler's wicket, the other at a position near square leg. Umpires are distinguishable by their white coats.

Wide The umpire will call a delivery a 'wide' if he considers it to be too high over, or too wide of, the stumps for the batsman to make contact with his bat from his normal stance. Like the no-ball, an extra delivery is made to replace the one delivered wide.

Wicket maiden An over in which the bowler concedes no runs and also takes at least one wicket. See also Maiden.

Yorker A delivery pitched well up and usually landing between the batsman's block hole and the base of the stumps.

So far you have learned how the game originated, what it is played with, and how to interpret the unique language of cricket. It is nearly time to get down to playing the game. But first, you must get to know the rules.

THE GAME – A GUIDE

Although the focal point of a game of cricket is the battle between bowler and batsman, there are eleven men in a team, and all play an important role.

Teams take it in turn to bat, and the batting team puts two of their men onto the playing area at one time. The other team, known as the fielding side, has all eleven of its players on the field.

It is well worth, at this stage, showing you the fielding positions and familiarizing you with the names of the fielders. You have most probably heard of such wonderfully named fielders as silly mid-on and short-leg, but where do they stand?

If you look at the diagram closely you will see there are thirty-four different fielding positions. I know I said there are only eleven players in a team, but the positions show the various options a fielder has to choose from. This is where good captaincy plays an important part. The captain will know the strengths and weaknesses of the opposing batsmen, and will instruct his fielders to occupy certain positions with that knowledge in mind.

The fielding side always take to the field first and are then followed by the first two batsmen of the opposing side – known as the 'openers', because they open the innings.

Also on the field there are two officials, known as umpires. They take up positions as shown. One is known as the bowler's umpire, the other as the square-leg umpire. Between them they have a clear view of most of the action and can readily make any ruling as is necessary. At this stage you ought to be told: *never argue with an umpire*. He is the sole arbitrator, and his decision is final. If he gives a batsman out, then he is out. All the arguing in the world will not do any good.

Right, so everybody is on the field and the captain has decided which man he wants to open the bowling, and from which end of the pitch. The receiving batsman asks the umpire for his guard and play commences with the first bowler delivering a ball to the receiving batsman.

The non-receiving batsman stands at the bowler's end of the pitch with his bat grounded in the popping crease.

The objective of the receiving batsman is to make a scoring stroke if possible; the objective of the bowler is to prevent such an action and attempt to dismiss the batsman. The forms of dismissal will be explained in greater detail shortly.

A scoring stroke results in runs being added to both the batsman's individual total and the team's aggregate total. Runs can also be added as a result of penalties. But these will be explained fully later.

The batsman can score runs by hitting the

Basic fielding positions

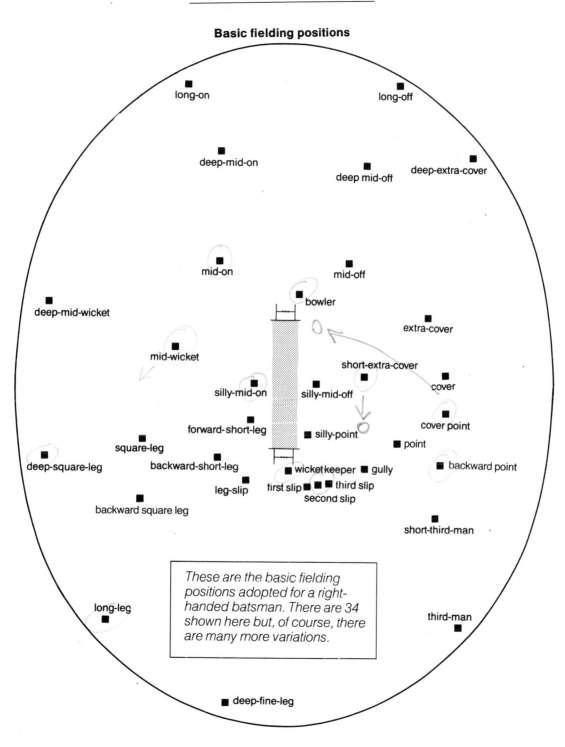

long-on

long-off

deep-mid-on

deep mid-off

deep-extra-cover

mid-on

mid-off

bowler

deep-mid-wicket

extra-cover

mid-wicket

short-extra-cover

silly-mid-on

silly-mid-off

cover

forward-short-leg

silly-point

cover point

square-leg

point

deep-square-leg

backward-short-leg

backward point

leg-slip

wicket keeper   gully

backward square leg

first slip   third slip
second slip

short-third-man

These are the basic fielding positions adopted for a right-handed batsman. There are 34 shown here but, of course, there are many more variations.

long-leg

third-man

deep-fine-leg

ball directly to the boundary. Any ball which crosses the boundary fence is worth four runs. If it passes the boundary without first touching the ground then it is worth six runs.

If the batsman makes a scoring stroke that does not reach the boundary, then the two batsmen must run between the wickets, and every time they both ground their bat in the opposite popping crease one run is added to the team score, and the batsman who made the scoring stroke is also individually credited with that score. Most runs actually *run* are singles, doubles or trebles. Occasionally four are run, but that is only on a large field where the boundary fence is some considerable distance from the wicket. Batsmen can, however, run as many runs as they want and are able.

Should an odd number of runs be run then the receiving batsman will change. The bowler continues his 'battle' with the batsman until he completes an over, which normally constitutes six deliveries, but local competition rules often vary this. The popular variant is an eight-ball over.

Once an over is completed, another bowler takes turns at bowling; the same man may not bowl consecutive overs. At the end of each over the batsmen remain at the same ends of the pitch; they do not change ends – it is the bowlers and other fielders who change ends. Therefore, if a player hit a single, or three runs, off the last ball of the over, he will retain the strike and take the first delivery of the next over from the new bowler.

Batsmen remain at the wicket until they are dismissed. Once dismissed, they leave the field and are replaced by a colleague. Once ten men have been dismissed (not eleven) the team innings comes to a close and the next team takes its turn to bat. The team scoring the most runs wins the match.

The duration of a match varies considerably according to local conditions. A local school match will often be concluded in an afternoon, with each side being allocated either a certain amount of time or

number of overs in which to score as many runs as possible. The latter is more practicable in view of the possibility of play being lost to adverse weather conditions. Rain, of course, is the biggest curse of the cricketer, but bad light is also a major problem because batsmen have great difficulty in following the flight or path of the ball in bad light.

At senior level the duration of matches also varies according to the type of competition. Test Matches last five days with a maximum of thirty hours play. County Championship matches are held over three or four days, while the Refuge Assurance League matches, Benson and Hedges Cup matches and National Westminster Bank Cup matches are all completed in one day. These last three are all limited over competitions and each side is allowed to bowl a maximum of forty, fifty-five and sixty overs respectively. In all cases the object is to score more runs than your opponents. In four-innings matches, the aggregate score of each sides' two innings are added together.

In limited over matches each side has one innings only, but in other matches teams either bat for one or two innings each.

Teams are allowed to declare their innings closed at any time during a match of four innings, thus trying to effect a result. For example, in the 1987 Somerset versus Glamorgan County Championship match at Weston-super-Mare, Glamorgan batted first and scored 351 runs for 9 wickets before declaring, Somerset replied by making 272 but declared their innings after the fall of the 5th wicket. Had they continued batting they could possibly have equalled or bettered Glamorgan's score but, as the match was based on the outcome of two innings, the chance of them winning was slim. So, they

West Indian Viv Richards plays a powerful off-drive between cover and mid-off. Note the follow-through and how he is keeping his eyes on the ball.

declared their first innings 79 runs short of Glamorgan's total.

Glamorgan then batted in their second innings and declared at 241 for 4. They had built up a lead of 320 runs and felt confident of dismissing all ten Somerset batsmen before they reached a winning score of 321. But how wrong they were: Somerset scored 321 runs for the loss of only three wickets and thus won the match. The outcome happened as a result of a good declaration by Somerset.

In that example, how many did Somerset win by? Trying to calculate the winning margin is often confusing to the newcomer to cricket.

The obvious result, one would think, is a Somerset win by one run, because they scored one run more than their opponents. But there again, Glamorgan lost thirteen wickets in all, Somerset lost only eight. So, did Somerset win by five wickets? No – they actually won by seven wickets! That is, the number of wickets they had left when they reached their match-winning total.

A simple rule when working out how many a team won by:

In *matches of four innings*, if the team who did **not** bat last wins, then their winning margin is the difference of runs between the two teams. If the team batting fourth wins, then the winning margin is the number of wickets they had left at the time of passing their opponents' overall score. In the above example, if Somerset had lost all their second innings wickets for 319 runs, then Glamorgan would have won by one run. If the scores are level and the side batting last still has wickets intact at the end of he match, it is declared a draw. If the scores are level and there are no wickets remaining, it is a tie.

In *limited over cricket* the same rules apply. If the winning team is the one which bats second, they win by the number of wickets they have intact. If the first batting side wins, they win by the number of runs margin.

That just about covers the rules in their basic form. We will be looking at them in closer detail in the **Rules Clinic** later on, but first we should look at the various methods of dismissal.

Bowled   A batsman is out bowled if his wicket is bowled 'down' or 'broken'. For that to happen the ball must touch a stump directly after being delivered from the bowler, or be played on to the wicket by the batsman after coming off either his bat or any part of his person. However, for the wicket to be down (or broken) one, or both, of the bails must be removed. The ball can hit the wicket and the bails remain in place. In such a case the batsman is not out.

Caught   A batsman is caught if the ball is caught by a fielder before it touches the ground after the ball has touched the bat or batman's hand, or glove, below the wrist that is holding the bat.

Timed out   An incoming batsman must step on to the field of play within two minutes of the last batsman being dismissed. If he does not, and the umpire believes the action was wilful, the batsman will be dismissed 'timed out'.

Handled the ball   A batsman can be given out 'handled the ball' if he wilfully handles the ball, while in play, with his hand not holding the bat, unless the opposite side consent to his touching it.

Hit the ball twice   If a batsman, after the ball is struck or stopped by any part of him, wilfully strikes the ball again, other than in trying to defend his wicket, he shall be given out 'hit the ball twice'.

Hit wicket   A batsman is out 'hit wicket' if he breaks his wicket with his bat or any part of his body or equipment while in the course of preparing for a shot, making a shot, or setting off on his first run.

Leg before wicket

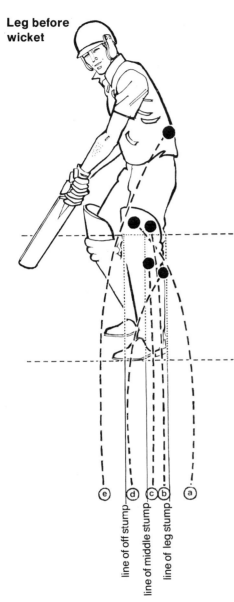

line of off stump

line of middle stump

line of leg stump

Leg before wicket Put simply, leg before wicket is the act of preventing the ball from hitting the wicket with any part of your body, not just the leg.

There are certain provisos with this form of dismissal, and the laws of the game distinguish according to whether the striker did or did not make an attempt to play the ball.

If the player does attempt to play the ball, and it does not touch his bat or hand holding the bat, he is out lbw if the ball hits any part of his body, provided:

(a) the ball is pitched in a straight line between the two sets of wickets, or

(b) the ball pitches on the off side of the striker's wicket, or

(c) if the ball hits the striker full pitch before hitting the ground, and it would have pitched in a straight line between the two sets of wickets. The point of impact between ball and striker must be in a straight line between the two sets of wickets, even if it is above the height of the bails.

If the striker makes no attempt to play the ball, he can still be out lbw provided the previous conditions are met, but he can also be given out even if the ball is intercepted outside the line of the off stump.

The diagram will clarify this often complex rule.

Obstructing the field If a batsman wilfully obstructs an opposing fielder, either by word or actions, he will be given out.

Run out When running between wickets the batsmen, as we have seen, must ground their bat in the opposite popping crease. They are said to have made good their ground. If, however, a member of the fielding side puts down the wicket before ground is made, the batsman is run out.

(a) *Is not out, any ball that pitches outside leg stump cannot warrant an lbw claim.*
(b) *Not out*
(c) *Out*
(d) *Doubtful, therefore not out*
(e) *Not out – would have bounced over the top of the stumps. Balls pitching on or about off stump, and moving into the batsman, depend more often than not on the umpire's discretion.*

CRICKET

Run out

This batsman has made good his ground.

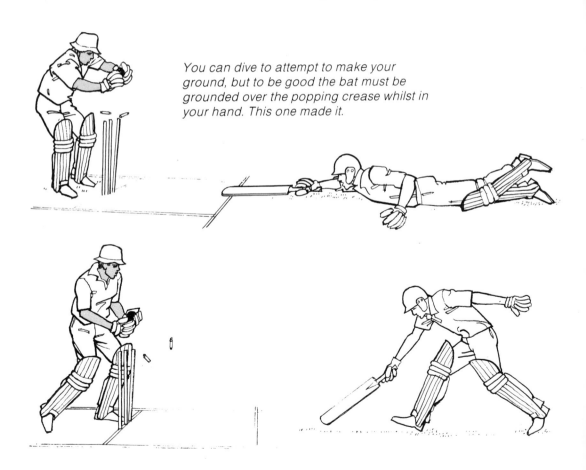

You can dive to attempt to make your ground, but to be good the bat must be grounded over the popping crease whilst in your hand. This one made it.

This batsman is run out.

Stumped   If the batsman is out of his ground and the wicket is put down by the wicketkeeper in the course of a stroke being made, the batsman is out 'stumped'. If the batsman is in the course of running and the wicketkeeper puts the wicket down, then he is not stumped, but run out.

Stumped

Having missed the ball the batsman is out of his ground and the quick-thinking wicketkeeper has stumped him.

Bowling offences

The bowler must make a lawful delivery. For it to be lawful it must comply with the following conditions:

(a) he must indicate to the umpire whether he intends bowling underarm or overarm (very rarely do you see underarm bowlers these days; underarm bowling is not permitted in limited overs cricket).

(b) whether he is to bowl round or over the wicket.

(c) whether he is to bowl right- or left-handed.

The ball must be bowled and not thrown. It is deemed to be a throw if all or part of the bowling arm is straightened during the part of the delivery immediately prior to the ball leaving the bowler's hand.

The bowler's feet also play an important part in his delivery. The back foot must be inside the return crease, and not touching its boundary. The front foot, either raised or grounded, must not be beyond the popping crease.

If the bowler contravenes any of these conditions his delivery shall be called a no-ball, and one run automatically added to the batting side's total if no runs are made as a result of the batsman's action. A no-ball does not count towards the over, and a replacement delivery has to be made.

A wide delivery is treated like a no-ball. One run is added if no runs result, and a replacement delivery is made in the over. A ball is deemed wide if it is so high above the batsman's head or wide of his reach when taking his normal guard, that he could not play a stroke.

Bowler's feet

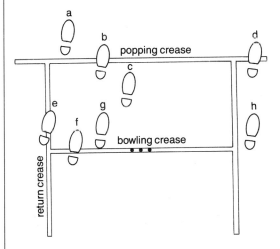

a, b, c and d represent the front foot.
b, c and d are legal.
a is a 'no-ball'.
e, f, g and h represent the back foot.
e and h are 'no-balls'.
f and g are legal, provided the corresponding front foot is legal.

Umpire's signals

The umpire uses a series of signals to give information to the official scorers. It also helps the spectators understand what is going on out on the pitch. To help you understand the game better the umpire's signals are as follows:

No-ball

Out

Boundary 6

Bye

Boundary 4

Wide

Short run

Dead ball

Leg bye

CRICKET

Extras

Wides and no-balls are classed as extras and are added to the team total. Extras are runs that are made other than with the bat. Other forms of extras are **byes** and **leg byes**.

A **bye** is a run, or runs, made after the ball passes the striker without touching his bat or person, and it has not been previously called a no-ball or wide. A **leg bye** is the same as the bye, but this time it is a run, or runs, made after the ball has struck the batsman or his clothing, other than his bat or hand holding the bat.

Note the close-in fielding positions for the right-hand off-break bowler. Gatting, at backward short leg, made the catch.

Scorecards

Cricket is a minefield of statistical information, and it lends itself to hours of fun playing around with figures if you are that way inclined. Most leading scorers develop their own forms of analysis, but most follow a traditional pattern of scoring which indicates the runs scored off each delivery, who scored them, how many balls have been bowled, the number of wickets fallen, and so on.

That's the rules and basic principles of cricket explained. Let us now look a bit more closely at some of those argumentative points which the laws of the game often produce . . .

RULES CLINIC

Do the fielders stand in the same position irrespective of whether the batsman is right- or left-handed?

No. The diagram on page 33 assumes the batsman to be right-handed. However, if he should be left-handed then fielders would stand on the opposite side of the pitch . . . as if it was a mirror-image.

Is a batsman automatically out if dismissed by one of the methods allowed in the laws of the game?

No. An umpire shall not give a player out unless a member of the fielding side appeals to the umpire. The appeal must be made before the bowler begins his run-up or bowling action of the next delivery. The appeal must be in the form of 'How's that?'

Does this mean that a bowler could have a player allegedly leg before wicket with the last ball of the day and the appeal could be made before the first ball of the next day?

Yes. And would you believe it, it *has* happened. The legendary W.G. Grace once did it.

Can a player leave the field at any time?

A fielder cannot leave the field without first gaining permission from the umpire at the bowler's end. If a substitute is necessary then, again, the umpire's permission is sought. A batsman can also leave the field of play if injured or due to illness, and he is replaced by the next batsman. However, at the fall of a wicket, within the same innings, the injured batsman may return.

You said the umpires stand at the bowler's wicket and at square-leg. Do they stand in these positions throughout the match?

No. At the end of each over the bowling umpire stays that end of the pitch but moves to square-leg, while the square-leg umpire takes up a position to become the bowling umpire at the other end. At the end of each innings they change ends.

How often is a new ball used in a match?

In a schools, club, or local parks match – not very often. It is normally a case of using the best available ball, not a question of using a new one. However, in the first-class game, a new ball can be used at the start of each innings subject to the agreement of the captains. In matches of three or more days a new ball is introduced after a prescribed number of overs. This figure varies from country-to-country, but must be a minimum of seventy-five. If a ball is lost or becomes unfit for play, the umpires will replace it with a ball which, in their opinion, has had a similar amount of wear.

What exactly is the follow-on?

In a two-innings-per-side match, the team batting second may be asked to follow-on and immediately bat in their second innings at the conclusion of their first innings if their total falls well short of the opening team's total. The deficits before the follow-on is introduced are usually:

5-or-more-day match:	200 run deficit
3/4-day match:	150 run deficit
2-day match:	100 run deficit
1-day match:	75 run deficit

What happens if the first day of a five-day match is lost due to bad weather? What is the follow-on deficit score then?

It would be 150, because it would be regarded as a four-day match if an entire day's play was lost.

Does a team have to send two batsmen on to the field to face one ball before making a declaration, or can they declare whilst still in the pavilion?

No. A captain may forfeit an innings rather than declare at 0 runs for 0 wickets, provided he notifies the opposing captain and umpires in good time.

What are the umpire's calls?

At the start of a day's play or an innings, or resumption after an interval, he calls 'play'. At the end of each over he calls 'over', and at the conclusion of a match, the end of a day's play, or the end of play before a break or interruption, he will call 'time'. If the ball is no longer in play he also calls 'dead ball'. He will call 'no-ball' and 'wide' if the bowler's delivery contravenes the laws accordingly.

If a batsman hits an almighty blow to the boundary and it is caught, but in the mean time a run has been completed, does the run count?

No.

If a batsman is run out, do the runs scored before the run-out count?

Yes – it is only the run being attempted that does not count. The same applies if a batsman is given out for obstructing the field, unless the obstruction prevents a fielder from making a catch.

If the batsmen complete a single run and then discover the ball has gone over the boundary, do they have to return to their original ends?

Yes. The batsman who scored the boundary re-takes the strike and the single run scored is *not* added to the score, just the four, or six, for the boundary. However, if they have run five runs and a boundary (four) is scored, then the five runs shall count provided they were completed by the time the ball crossed the boundary. Mind you, it would need to be a big boundary for two batsmen to run five in the time it takes the ball to hit it!

Australian bowler, Craig McDermott, brings strength and determination to his bowling and firmly established himself as his country's front-line strike bowler in the early 1990s.

CRICKET

You said the umpire announces when the over is completed by calling 'over', but what happens if he miscalculates the number of balls delivered?

The number of deliveries as counted by the umpire shall stand.

Can the non-striking batsman stand the same side of the wicket as the bowler?

No, unless agreed by the umpire in exceptional circumstances. He must stand the opposite side of the wicket from which the bowler makes his delivery.

Is it only the bowler who can have a 'no-ball' called against him?

No. A fielder or wicketkeeper can have a delivery called a no-ball if he infringes any of the laws.

Can runs be scored off a no-ball?

Yes, they can, and any runs scored are credited to the batsman and debited to the bowler. Byes and leg byes scored are extras. If no runs are scored with the bat, then one penalty run is added to the team score (not the batsman's), and is not debited to the bowler's figures.

Can a batsman be out off a no-ball?

Yes, but only for hitting the ball twice, obstructing the field, handling the ball or run out. A batsman cannot be out bowled, caught, leg before wicket, hit wicket or stumped.

Can a batsman be out from a wide ball?

Yes, but only for handling the ball, hitting wicket, stumped, run out or obstructing the field.

Are byes and leg byes included in the bowler's analysis?

No.

Can a boundary be scored off a bye or leg bye?

Yes.

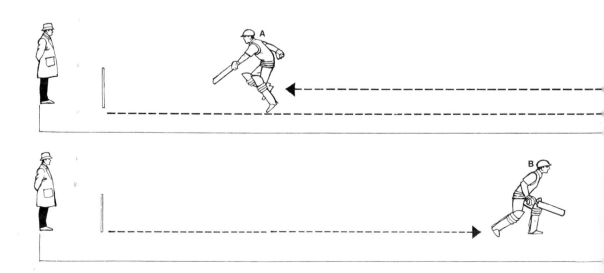

When is a batsman adjudged to be in his ground?

If some part of the bat in his hand, or part of his person, is grounded behind the line of the popping crease. The bat cannot be thrown into the crease in order to make ground; it must be held.

If a delivery hits the batsman's pad in what would be an lbw decision, and then hits the wicket, is he out lbw or bowled?

You obviously weren't paying attention earlier! He is bowled.

A ball hits a fielder on the head and is caught by another fielder before touching the ground. Is the batsman out?

Yes. However, if the fielder whose head got in the way was wearing a protective helmet, the catch would not be legal. On the plus side, at least the fielder wouldn't have a headache . . .

Can a player be out hit wicket if he hits the stumps while running?

He can if he breaks the wicket while setting off on his first run, but if he breaks the wicket in the normal course of running, or in avoiding a run out or a returned ball, he cannot be given out.

Once a batsman has completed his run and made ground, does he have to stay in his ground?

No. He can get out of the way to avoid any thrown balls, or just wander away from his ground, if he so wishes. He must return to his ground before the next delivery.

In a run out, which batsman is out?

If the batsmen have crossed then the one running to the wicket put down is out. If they have not crossed then the batsman who left the wicket put down is out. If one batsman remains in his ground, or returns to it, and the other batsman joins him, then the last-named is out if his wicket is put down.

In the top example batsman 'B' is out because the two men have crossed. In the bottom example, it is batsman 'A' who is out because they have not crossed.

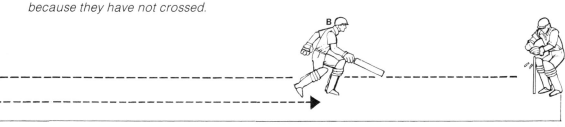

If a fielder prevents a boundary being scored and then touches the boundary fence with his foot, is the stroke classed as a boundary?

Yes. If he touches or grounds any part of his person on or over the boundary fence with a ball in his hands, he forfeits the boundary. You can, however, stop the ball inside the boundary, and then run over the boundary fence. This is allowed provided you do not have the ball in your hand at the time.

If a player catches a ball and then steps over the boundary, is it still a six?

Yes. It is also still a six if the ball touches the fielder on its way to passing over the boundary without first hitting the ground.

If the batsmen run as a result of an overthrow, are the overthrows regarded as extras or are they credited to a batsman?

They are credited to the receiving batsman.

What happens if an overthrow reaches the boundary?

The value of the boundary shall be added to the runs already run. The run in progress shall count provided the batsmen have crossed.

Where must protective helmets be put when not being worn?

Behind the wicketkeeper. If a ball, while in play, strikes the helmet, then five penalty runs are added to the batting team's score.

In the event of a lost ball, is the batting side credited with any runs?

Yes. At the moment the fielder announces 'lost ball' six runs are added. However, if the fielders have run more than six then the higher total shall count. Obviously, if the ball

crosses a boundary before it is lost then only the runs scored for the boundary shall count. You won't see this happen in the senior game, but playing on the local park there is every chance it will happen quite often. Mind you, you could do with keeping an eye on that ball – they are not cheap to replace.

You said earlier that in limited over matches the team scoring the most runs wins, but how come I have seen teams with fewer runs become the winning side?

This happens if a match is curtailed because of the weather. The team with the better run rate, provided both teams have received twenty overs, is declared the winner.

Does the bowler get credit for all types of dismissals?

No. He only gets credit for batsmen bowled, caught, stumped, leg before wicket and hit wicket.

What happens if it is so windy the bails won't stay on the wicket?

The umpire has the power to remove them and use his discretion in deciding when the wicket is down.

Can a fielder throw his cap at the ball to stop it?

No. If he does, then five penalty runs shall be added. Any runs already made shall also count. A fielder must stop the ball only with any part of his person.

If five penalty runs are added to a team's score, do the batsmen have to change ends because an odd number of runs have been 'scored'?

No, they stay in their same ground.

Limited over matches fielding positions

A minimum of 4 fielders, plus the bowler and wicketkeeper must be within the marked area at the moment of delivery, otherwise a 'no-ball' is called. White disks spaced at 5-yd (4.57m) intervals mark the fielding area.

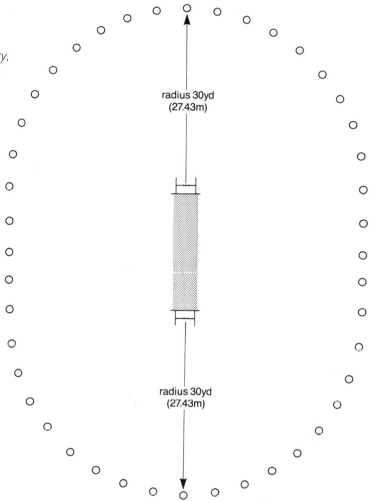

radius 30yd
(27.43m)

radius 30yd
(27.43m)

Are there any restrictions on the placement of fielders?

Yes. The wicketkeeper must stand behind the wicket until the ball is either hit, hits the batsman, or passes the wicket. Also, the number of on-side fielders behind the popping crease at the moment of the delivery shall not exceed two.

From the moment the ball comes into play until the moment it is hit or passes the batsman's bat, no fielder may stand or have any part of his body on or over the pitch.

In limited over competitions, rules dictate how many fielders may stand close-in. At the moment of delivery, a minimum of four fielders (excluding the bowler and wicketkeeper) must be within a specially marked area. (See diagram.)

TECHNIQUE

C ricket technique falls into three distinct categories: bowling, batting and fielding. Let's start with bowling.

BOWLING

Before we look at the different styles of bowling, a brief examination of the ball will prove worthwhile.

You regularly see bowlers rubbing the ball on their trousers. They do this to try and keep it as shiny as possible. A shiny ball will come off the pitch faster and higher than a well-used one. At the beginning of a match, therefore, it is advantageous to use fast bowlers who can get the maximum benefit from a new, and therefore shinier, ball because of their extra pace.

The seam on the ball also plays an important role. By presenting the seam in a particular way at the moment of delivery, the ball can be made to change direction, either on pitching, or in the air. A ball might turn in flight simply because of air conditions, or because the bowler has used the seam to the same effect. The seam can also cause the ball to deviate once it pitches. It therefore makes sense to try and get the ball to pitch on the seam, as this will always help to make the batsman's job harder.

You will see many varied bowling styles as you watch different bowlers in action. Some may be fast, some slow, and some medium-paced. We will look at all the different bowling styles and techniques later in this chapter. But, no matter what style a bowler adopts, he should always bear the following fundamental points in mind:

(a) a sound grip of the ball;
(b) a good run-up to the wicket;
(c) a nice smooth delivery;
(d) a fluent follow-through.

The grip

We will look at the different forms of grip later as we look at each individual style, but first of all you should familiarize yourself with the basic grip. The important thing to remember is: *hold the ball with your fingers, not in the palm of the hand*.

The run-up

The length of the run-up depends on the pace at which you want to deliver the ball.

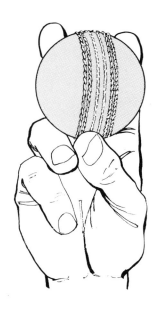

The basic grip

wicket too soon, or too late, alter the position of the marker. Practice run-ups are permitted, and are recommended.

When you begin your run-up, you should fix your eyes firmly on the intended flight of the ball, or the point where you intend the ball to pitch, and keep them fixed there throughout the run-up. Be careful not to run up too fast, and, more importantly, make sure the run-up is fluent.

The delivery

When you first reach the wicket, your left shoulder should be pointing down the wicket at the batsman, and your left arm above your head. At this point the weight is on the back foot (the right) but as the delivery is effected, the weight is transferred to the front foot (the left) and the trunk turned so that it is facing the opposite wicket. As the bowling arm (right) is swung forward, the left arm makes a move in the opposite direction, giving a windmill-like effect. At the point of delivery the back foot is raised off the ground ready to commence the follow-through.

Usually the longer the run-up, the faster the bowler's delivery. Before commencing bowling, you should pace out the number of strides it will take from the wicket to the point where your run-up commences. You should mark that point to make sure your run-up is consistent. If you find you are arriving at the

Run up

Note the eyes fixed on the target. Just before the delivery both feet are off the ground. Try and keep the head as still as possible and achieve a good follow-through.

Delivery

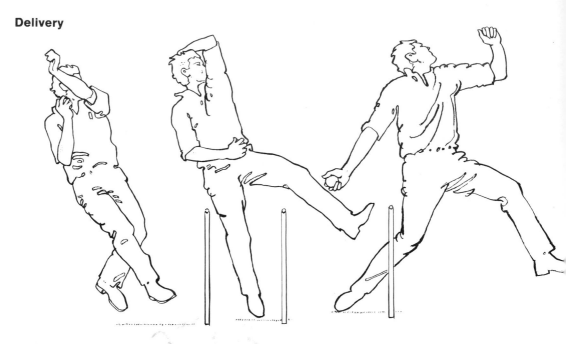

The follow-through

The pace of the delivery will dictate the length of follow-through, and natural momentum will cause the bowler to take a few extra strides down the pitch after delivering the ball. However, in an effort not to damage the pitch, any follow-through strides should be made to the side of the pitch.

These are the basics of bowling, but there is a great deal more to it.

A good bowler will know the batsman he is bowling to. If he doesn't, then he should spend a few overs observing his style of play. For example, does he like to play shots off his front foot or his back foot? Once you know your 'opponent', you should bowl accordingly and make life as tough as possible for him. It is therefore important to alter your length of delivery, thus introducing the element of surprise and so preventing the batsman from getting settled in at the wicket.

The key to successful bowling is accuracy. If you regularly deliver accurate balls on a good length, then the batsman's job becomes increasingly more frustrating. Being able to vary your length will confuse the batsman; he will become uncertain whether to play off his front or back foot. Uncertainty is disastrous for a batsman.

If your fielders compliment your bowling as you perform, then the batsman will get even more frustrated. The batsman's job is to score runs. If he is not doing so, he will inevitably start taking risks. That is when he becomes more vulnerable. So *concentrate on making sure your bowling is accurate first and foremost*. Pace is unimportant provided you are accurate.

Correct fielding positions are important for each type of delivery. It is up to the bowler and his captain to decide the best fielding positions. We will outline the positions in greater detail in the **FIELDING** section.

Fast bowlers should make sure they are suitably warmed-up before bowling. Tight muscles are no good to a fast bowler. Deliveries are likely to be wild, and furthermore, there is the risk of injury.

TECHNIQUE

Above: *Front view of the moment of delivery.*

Follow-through

Note how the bowler moves to the left and away from the pitch so as not to cause any damage.

Let us now look at some different types of delivery:

Swing bowling

A swing bowler will cause the ball to move in mid-air. A ball will move in flight because of air, wind, and air-pressure. The direction the seam points, and the amount of polish on a ball, will also dictate its flight path.

There are two types of ball one can deliver with swing bowling: the **inswinger** and the **outswinger**.

The **inswinger** moves in the air and cuts across the batsman, and away down the leg-side. To gain maximum swing, only the half of the ball facing the leg side should be shined, and the ball gripped with the seam pointing towards leg side. The fingers on top

of the ball should be close together, and the thumb supporting the seam. When making the delivery the bowler should stand slightly to the side of the wicket. The point of aim is on, or slightly outside, off stump. After pitching it will swing in towards the wicket.

The **outswinger** is the opposite. It swings in the air to the off side. The best place for it to pitch is on middle and off, and bowled with a full length. This time the inner side of the ball should be shined and the seam should point approximately towards first slip. The thumb is placed underneath the seam and the two top fingers are placed either side of the seam. The outswinger is a useful delivery against a batsman who has a liking for playing shots down the leg side, as it prevents him from making a shot of this kind easily and increases the likelihood of his

Inswinger

Note the high point of delivery.

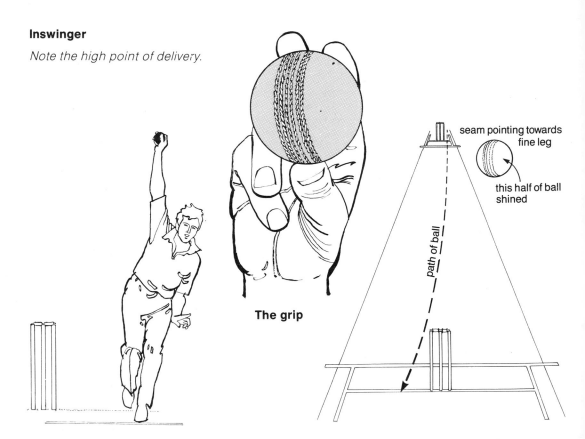

The grip

seam pointing towards fine leg

this half of ball shined

Path of ball

The outswinger

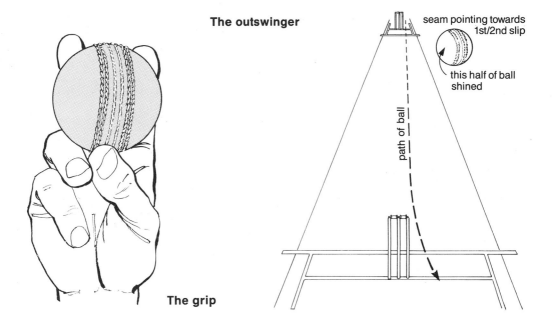

seam pointing towards
1st/2nd slip

this half of ball
shined

path of ball

The grip

'edging' a ball to the wicketkeeper or the slips.

A point worth remembering with all swing deliveries, *the nearer the striker's wickets the ball pitches the greater chance there is of it swinging.*

Spin bowling

A good spinner is a treat to watch. Sadly, there is a shortage of good quality spin bowlers in the senior game these days.

Spinners use the pitch to its fullest in effecting spin. But they must firstly adopt the correct grip for each type of delivery. A good spinner will be able to vary his delivery and will confuse the opposing batsman.

If you decide you want to develop a good spinning technique, then you ought to spend time developing the spin aspect of the actual delivery. Once you have mastered that, and can see what happens to the ball after it pitches, then you want to develop your accuracy of length and direction. With spin bowling, it is not pace that counts, but accuracy.

Off-spin The ball will pitch on the off side and spin in towards the wicket. If bowled round the wicket the path of the ball and spin will be exaggerated even further.

The ball is gripped with the tips of the first and second fingers placed on the seam. The further apart you can get your fingers, the greater the spin will be. The thumb plays no part in the delivery.

When making the delivery it is important to have the palm of the hand facing upwards at the bottom of the bowling action. As the hand is brought up, the wrist and fingers twist clockwise and carry on doing so until after the ball has left the hand.

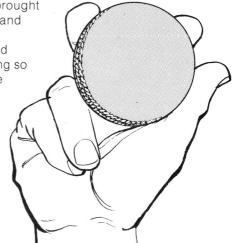

Off-spin

This action imparts the spin. The ball should be released from a high position, approximately when the delivery arm becomes level with the bowler's head.

If the pitch is not taking spin, then this type of delivery should be made over the wicket and aimed to pitch just outside the off stump. If the pitch is taking a lot of spin then round-the-wicket bowling will create greater spin and more problems for the batsman, but will reduce the chances of getting an lbw decision. Depending upon the amount of spin the wicket is taking, the bowler can create even more problems for the batsman by varying his bowling position. In other words, by utilizing the full width of the bowling crease and by flighting the ball not bowling with a flat trajectory.

Leg-break spin   The leg-break is a spin action that moves from leg to off after pitching. It is effected by causing the ball to spin in an anti-clockwise direction.

The ball is gripped with it resting on the base of the thumb and with the first and second fingers spaced out on top of the ball and along the seam. The third finger supports the ball similarly to the base of the thumb.

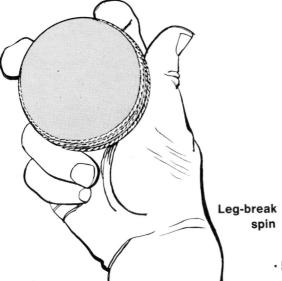

Leg-break spin

A leg-break bowler will often use the basic delivery action, but it is what he does with his wrist at the moment of delivery that is all important.

At the bottom of the bowling action the wrist is bent forward with the fingers pointing towards the opposite wicket. As the arm is brought up to its delivery position, the wrist is twisted anti-clockwise and the ball 'flipped' out of the hand.

Leg-break deliveries should be made from over the wicket. Varying length and flight are important for a leg-break bowler. Because he cannot claim a victim lbw if the ball pitches outside the line of the leg-stump, it is important to bowl accurately at the stumps.

The googly is a form of leg-break delivery. The grip is the same as that of the conventional leg-break, but the back of the hand is upright at the moment the ball is delivered, thus imparting off-spin. The ball should be pitched at off stump, or outside.

The googly is a leg-break in disguise and should be used not on its own but amongst leg-break deliveries, to provide variation.

Bouncer   The bouncer is a fast, short-pitched, ball which bounces up to the batsman at at least chest height. It should not be used as a regular delivery but, again, as a form of surprise, particularly against the batsman who appears to be getting settled in at the wicket. It should be made down the on side in the hope of getting the batsman to make contact, but preventing him from making a hook.

Within the spirit of the game bouncers should not be delivered against poor batsmen. Against better batsmen however, the bouncer is regarded as just another of the deliveries that form part of the intriguing battle between bowler and batsman.

The ball that possibly gets the best batsmen out is the ball that goes away to the slips, i.e. left-hand spinner, leg-break and outswinger.

BATTING

Now that you understand the job of the bowler, and how he tries to gain the initiative, we will look at the batsman's role, and see how he tries to counteract the bowler and turn each delivery into a scoring stroke.

Just as the bowler has his basics, so does the batsman. The following are vital for successful batting:

(a) good grip;
(b) good stance, including good head and body positions;
(c) good footwork.

The bat must be gripped firmly by both hands. Many people tend to forget about the top hand and rely on the bottom hand to do all the gripping. The two hands should grip the bat near the top of the handle, not low down. The fingers, and thumbs, should be well-wrapped around the handle. As you grip, each hand will form a 'V' with the thumb and first finger. The 'V' of the top

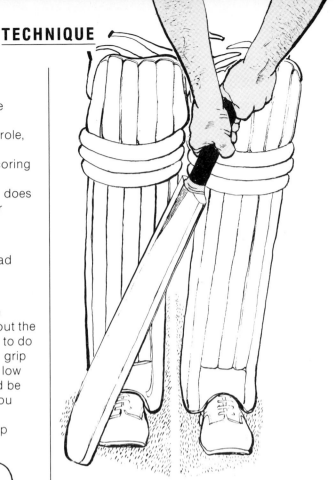

The grip

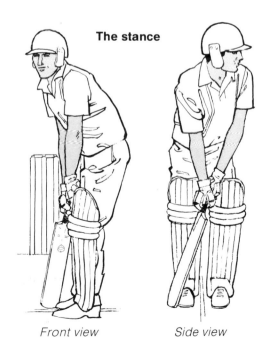

The stance

Front view   *Side view*

hand should be parallel with the 'V' formed by the lower hand.

The purpose of a good stance is to enable the batsman to get into position easily and quickly for every type of stroke. The correct stance is adopted by taking up a sideways-on position with the left shoulder facing the bowler and the face of the bat pointing down the wicket.

The feet should not be too far apart, and one placed either side of the popping crease. Your body weight should be equally distributed between the two feet, and not all on your heels. When grounding the bat in the normal stance position, the end should be positioned just behind the back foot, and the hands should rest on the top of the pad. It is important to keep your head up, and the

eyes firmly fixed on the ball.

The first movement in any batting stroke is the **backlift**, the moment when you take the bat away from its grounded position to a raised position ready to make the stroke. The backlift is carried out by the top hand alone. As the bat is lifted upwards the wrists are cocked and consequently the bat face becomes open. The key to a good backlift is *keep it straight, and fluent*.

Batting is not only about making scoring strokes. There are times when it is not possible to score a run off a delivery. It is therefore vitally important to be able to play defensive strokes as well.

The key to successful batting is having the ability to read a delivery, and being able to decide quickly how best to play the stroke. For example, should it be played off the front foot or the back foot? Decisions like this appear to be difficult to the newcomer, but in no time you will find yourself making such a decision without thinking about it. The best way to educate the brain in such matters is to spend hours of practice in the 'nets', a practice area available on most cricket grounds.

Before we look at the attacking strokes we will study the defensive stroke.

The defensive stroke

This is played with the front foot forward, the head and left shoulder well forward, and with a bent front knee. The stroke is controlled by the left arm. The bat face is kept square and makes contact with the ball level with the front foot. The ball is effectively stopped dead and will move only a small distance from the bat.

The back defensive stroke is another defensive stroke, but this time played off the back foot, and with the batsman in a position not dissimilar to his original stance.

This shot is played to a delivery that is slightly short of a length and will hit the bat roughly at bail-height. The face of the bat is square to the delivery and the ball played down. A follow-through is not necessary.

Now for the attacking shots . . .

TECHNIQUE

Forward defensive stroke

Lead with the head and front shoulder on to the line of the ball, the front foot will then automatically get into the correct position. The head must be steady and the legs as level as possible. See how the left leg is brought forward and bent at the knee: the stroke is played with the left hand and arm.

Back defensive stroke

Lead with the head and shoulder, keep your eyes on the ball and bat-face square.

The drive

You don't have to wait for the ball to pitch before making the drive, you can move down the wicket to meet the ball.

The drive

An effective shot, it is also one of the game's most delightful strokes if played correctly. There are three kinds of drive: (i) the off-drive; (ii) the on-drive; and (iii) the straight drive.

The off-drive   As its name implies, it is a ball driven to the off side of the field. The ball will be pitched on or outside off stump. The eye must be firmly fixed on the ball, and contact should be made with the ball when it is level with the front foot. The front foot should be advanced and as near to the pitch of the ball as possible. The front foot points towards cover and your weight is transferred to the front foot. Good balance and follow-through are crucial in a good drive, and remember, make sure that front

foot is level with the ball when it pitches. The face of the bat should be square to the intended line of the stroke.

The on-drive   This time the drive is made to the on side of the field. Typical of strokes made off the front foot, the head and shoulders are initially the dominant parts of the body. They lead forward, followed by the front foot and then the arms and the bat.

The front foot is this time pointing more towards mid-off. The face of the bat must be kept square with the intended line of stroke yet again.

The straight drive   This shot is no different, except the ball is hit between the bowler and mid-off. If the ball is met a bit earlier than normal (further in front of the front foot) the ball will be driven with loft. The follow-through after the straight drive sees the body rise after making contact. Of course there is the danger of being caught from the straight drive hit over the bowler's head.

We have said that drives should be made by making contact with the ball when it is level with the front foot. However, it is still possible to make a drive from a short-pitched ball. It means the batsman must advance down the pitch to meet it.

The principles are the same as for the other drives, but this time the batsman must first move the left foot forward, then bring the right foot up to it before the left foot is advanced again, this time to meet the pitch of the ball. It is not possible to play such a stroke unless the delivery is slow and the ball is given plenty of flight. The batsman could not get into position otherwise.

Moving down the pitch to play the drive requires confidence. One false move and you could well be out, either bowled or stumped.

Off the back foot

We saw earlier how a defensive shot is played off the back foot. However, time permitting, an equally effective attacking shot can be made off the back foot.

The best time to play a shot off the back foot is against a ball pitched short of a length which is pitched on, or just outside, the line of the stumps.

To play the shot, the batsman takes the right foot back towards, and parallel to, the stumps, still leading with the head and shoulder in line. This gives the batsman more chance to play the attacking stroke. All the weight is taken on the back foot. A lot of the power comes from the lower hand, which pushes the stroke forward. The bat, as usual, points towards the direction of the stroke. Make sure your backlift is high enough.

Playing off the back foot

Make sure you step far enough back, and across, the wicket – but not too far!

Playing the full toss

Timing and keeping your eye on the ball are the keys to successfully playing the full toss – not all full tosses are down the leg side like the one illustrated here. If the ball is bowled to off-side you hit to off-side. If it is bowled directly at the stumps you must play it with a straight back.

Playing the full toss

A full toss is a delivery that does not bounce before it reaches the bat. The best way to play it is to strike it to the leg side.

As the ball doesn't pitch, it is important to keep your eye on the ball during its flight. The head and front leg come forward and from a high backswing the bat is brought across the body to make the stroke. Contact with the ball should be at a point near to the extent of the outstretched arms.

To make sure the ball is hit down, the bottom hand should roll over the other hand at the point of contact, and after making the stroke the blade of the bat should be facing the floor.

Pull

The pull is a stroke played to a delivery which pitches on or outside the leg stump, and is pulled away to the leg side of the field. It should only be attempted if the delivery is short of a length. Anticipation and early judgement are essential.

As soon as you have decided the pull is

the shot to make, both feet should be taken well back. At the same time the bat should be taken back in a high backswing. As the bat is brought down to make the stroke the left leg is moved to the on side, which results in the chest being opened square to the bowler. The weight is gradually transferred to the left leg, and, at contact, the right wrist turns slightly over the left which will help in keeping the ball down.

Hook

Unlike the pull, the hook is made off the back foot, and is a lofted shot. It is played to a faster short-pitched ball and is hit when the ball is about chest high.

Again, a high backlift is important, and it is important to get the feet into position in order to have as much time as possible to read the ball after pitching.

Sweep

The sweep is a pull to the leg-side to a slower delivery which pitches outside the leg stump. Unlike the pull, however, it is made in

a crouching position, and the ball is struck when close to the ground.

The front foot comes down the wicket to meet the ball, but is then bent. The back leg is bent completely with the knee touching, or virtually touching, the ground. The ball is pulled away with the bat almost horizontal to the floor.

Cut

Unlike the drive, the cut is made to an under-pitched ball wide of the off stump. Being under-pitched, the batsman has plenty of time to sight the ball and get into position.

The back foot is taken across the stumps and the weight transferred onto it. The high backlift turns the shoulders. The ball is struck with the bat almost at arm's length and with the end of the blade dipping slightly. This effects the downward stroke and thus reduces the chance of a slip catch. The stroke is played with a downward movement on to the ball.

Glances

The two forms of glance, the forward leg glance and the backward leg glance, are similar to their forward and backward defensive counterparts.

In the forward glance, the front foot is brought inside the line of the ball. At the moment of impact the wrists are cocked to enable the ball to be turned away.

With the backward leg glance the back foot is moved nearer to the stumps; the front foot is also moved backwards. These movements of the feet are necessary as a result of the ball being pitched just short of a length, which is the the ideal time to play a shot like this. At the moment the bat makes contact with the ball (about bail-high), the hands turn the bat to the direction of the intended stroke.

Running between the wickets

Once a scoring stroke has been made (or a bye or leg bye called), and the ball does not reach the boundary, then the two batsmen have to run between the wickets and

successfully ground their bats every time they reach the opposite popping crease.

Successful running depends on good liaison and understanding between the batsmen. One should always call and advise the other whether a run is 'on' or not by calling either 'yes' or 'no' or wait.

The striker is generally responsible for the call if he hits the ball in front of the wicket. If it goes behind the wicket it is the non-striker's responsibility. Make sure you are positive with your call. Once the run has started there is very rarely any 'turning back'.

The decision to run a second or third run is generally left to the batsman who is most likely to be put out, often the one running to the wicket nearest to where the ball is being fielded. If there is a danger of a run-out, then there is nothing to stop you diving along the ground in an effort to get your bat grounded in the crease. Don't be frightened of getting your clothes dirty, they can always be washed!

Don't forget though – not all deliveries have to be hit, or even attempted, by the batsman. You can leave the ball to pass the wicket. You must, however, make sure that if a ball is left you are not going to be bowled out or leg before wicket. Sometimes there is not enough time to think about it . . . that is when the bowler usually has the last say!

You will have gathered from all the foregoing that timing, balance, feet positioning, and keeping your eye on the ball are vital factors in every stroke. Don't ever forget them. They will become second nature in time. But, until they do, many hours spent in the nets will do nothing but good for your game.

Graham Gooch shows great concentration in performing the full range of cricketing skills. Whether he is batting, bowling, fielding or taking captaincy decisions, his application is apparent and impressive.

FIELDING

It is pointless having good batsmen and bowlers in a side if they are not complemented by good fielders. Poor fielders cost runs, poor fielders cost wickets.

A good team will consist of maybe three or four top-class bowlers, three or four top-class batsmen and *eleven* good-class fielders.

Fielders should be fit and agile, able to read situations and, of course, be good catchers and retrievers of the ball . . .

Fielders spend long hours out on the field of play, and some stand around for quite a while before they are called into action. This is where they must have the ability to maintain their concentration.

The two main objectives of the fielder are (i) to prevent runs, and (ii) to assist in the taking of wickets.

Close-in fielders should be stooped and ready for any catches.

Fielding

Left and below: get your body behind the ball when stopping it.

To *prevent runs* they must be able to get to a ball as quickly as possible and return it to either wicket equally as quickly. There is no finer sight than an alert fielder collecting a ball while on the run and in the same continuous movement returning the ball to the wicket. But that sort of top-class fielder has spent many years developing his particular skill.

Often, a fielder has to chase after a ball with his back to the action. He must, while chasing the ball, picture his position in relation to the wickets, and must also build a mental picture of what is happening behind him because, the moment he gathers the ball, he must turn around and throw it to one of the wickets. He will receive a call from either a fielder at the bowler's wicket or the wicketkeeper at the other end, telling him which wicket to throw to in an attempt to get a fielder run out.

When retrieving the ball near to the wicket, an underarm return aimed at the stumps can often get the batsman run out.

Returning a fielded ball.

Fielding positions: 1

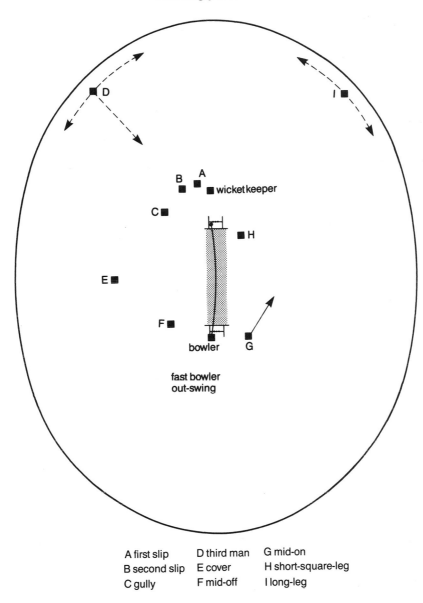

A first slip   D third man   G mid-on
B second slip   E cover   H short-square-leg
C gully   F mid-off   I long-leg

Possible field for a fast bowler bowling outswingers.

CRICKET

Fielding positions: 2

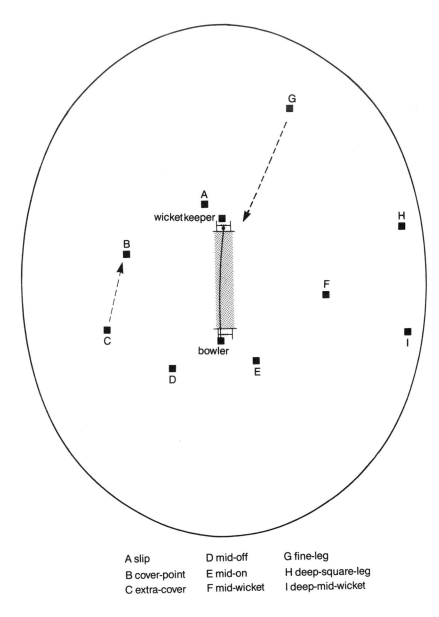

A slip	D mid-off	G fine-leg
B cover-point	E mid-on	H deep-square-leg
C extra-cover	F mid-wicket	I deep-mid-wicket

A typical field setting for an off-spin bowler. Note how most of the fielders are now on the on side.

Fielding positions: 3

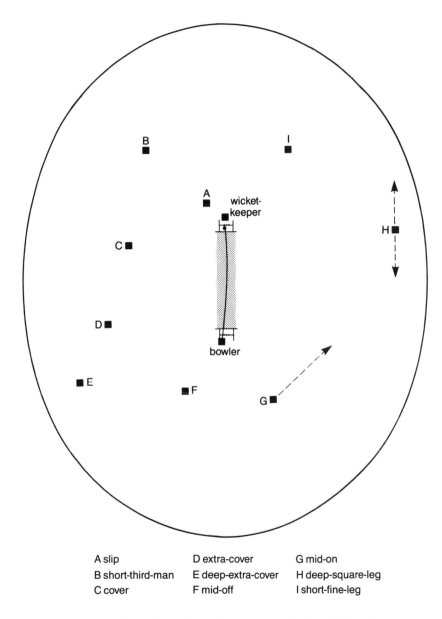

A slip	D extra-cover	G mid-on
B short-third-man	E deep-extra-cover	H deep-square-leg
C cover	F mid-off	I short-fine-leg

This setting is for a leg-spinner. If the pitch is taking a lot of turn then short third man (B) will take up a position of 2nd slip next to (A).

CRICKET

Fielding positions: 4

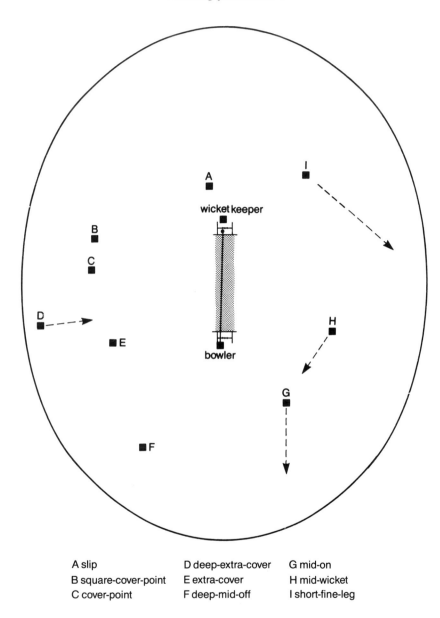

A slip	D deep-extra-cover	G mid-on
B square-cover-point	E extra-cover	H mid-wicket
C cover-point	F deep-mid-off	I short-fine-leg

This setting is for a slow left-arm bowler. Note this time how many fielders are well away from the pitch, ready to collect the ball in the deep.

Fielding positions: 5

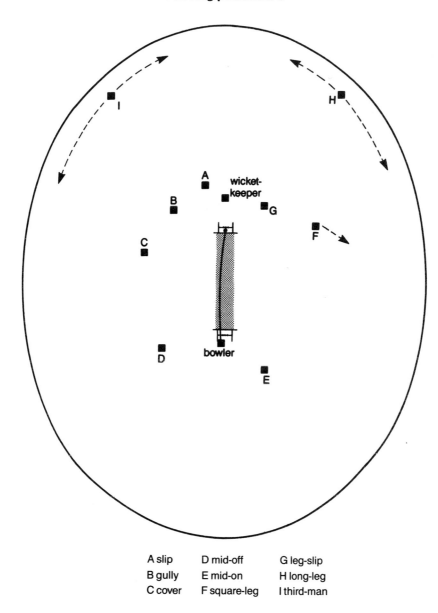

A slip	D mid-off	G leg-slip
B gully	E mid-on	H long-leg
C cover	F square-leg	I third-man

A typical setting for a medium-paced bowler delivering inswingers. All these settings are a guide only. Each bowler and captain will have his own preferences and, of course, how the batsman plays is important in deciding the field placings.

When catching a ball, the hands should be kept together and the eyes firmly fixed on the ball right up to the moment the ball lands in your hands. If you are out on the boundary and a ball is hit into the air, you should judge the flight of the ball before moving into position to make the catch. If anything, 'under-read' the flight, because it is easier to move forwards at the last moment in an effort to make the catch than it is to try to take the catch while running backwards.

The wicketkeeper

The wicketkeeper is a most important player when his team are in the field. He can watch for the batsman's strengths and weaknesses and confer with his captain and bowler generally on how to combat the opposition and actively prevent them making runs and assist in dismissals – either by making catches, stumpings or run outs.

The 'keeper must either stand up to the stumps for the slow bowler and (if a better-than-average wicketkeeper) also to the medium pacers, or stand back to the fast bowlers. Close liaison between 'keeper and bowler is imperative. He should be in a comfortable squat position with the knees bent and feet spread, the head perfectly still and eyes level, hands together, fingers pointing towards the ground. He must ensure a position with a clear view of the bowler throughout his run-up and delivery.

Fingers must point down when taking the ball and the hands must give, letting the ball come to the body, not snatching at it. The ball should be taken with the strongest hand when taking catches on the off- and leg-side. If the ball is above shoulder height the fingers should point to 12 o'clock – the

After progressing through schools, youth and county cricket, Alec Stewart has made the most of his opportunities at Test level and is clearly being groomed as a future England captain.

fingers must *never* be pointing at the ball.

When he stands up to the stumps the 'keeper must stay down, head perfectly still, until the bowler's delivery has pitched. He should always try to get both cupped hands behind the ball. If right-handed the ball should come in to the right hand first.

Concentration and watching the ball are the main requirements when standing back to the fast bowler, positioning himself to take the ball at waist level.

Once a scoring stroke has been made the 'keeper must run up to the wicket as quickly as possible and be ready to receive the throw ins. He must be aware of where the two batsmen are and advise the fielder to which end he should throw. The common faults in wicketkeeping are loss of concentration, taking the eyes off the ball and getting up too early from the crouched position.

The wicketkeeper

Crouched and ready for the next delivery.

The wicketkeeper

Upright and waiting to collect a fielded ball: note how he collects the ball and in a continuous movement carries on the stumps for a possible run out.

We have looked at the bowlers, the batsmen and the fielders. But there is one other important member of a team. He is the man who brings all the players together on the field: the captain.

The role of the captain

Good captains don't necessarily have to be outstanding players. Likewise, outstanding players don't always make good captains. Mike Brearley and Ian Botham are two recent England captains who, respectively, prove those rules very well. However, there is no doubting the value of a good captain on the playing field.

A good captain is a man who knows the strength and weaknesses of his own team and those of the opposition. He knows how to position his field, not only in relation to a particular batsman, but taking into account how he will react to a particular bowler.

Cricket is a well-disciplined game, and the captain should make sure such discipline, and the spirit of the game, is upheld at all times. Leading by example is the best way for a captain to do this. A good captain will also instil a great feeling of confidence and team spirit. Ultimately, that can only lead to a winning team.

Apart from helping with team selection, one of the most difficult decisions a captain has to make before a match begins is, 'Do we bat or bowl if we win the toss?' Points the captain has to take into consideration when making this decision are: the state of the pitch, which is normally at its best early in the game; the strength and weaknesses of the opposition; the fitness of his bowlers; what weather is expected; and the type of competition being played in. After that lot, the skipper has to decide whether to bat or field first! Is it hardly surprising that occasionally they get it wrong?

Some captains have a great knack for knowing where to place fielders for particular bowlers. As a match comes to its conclusion, particularly a one-day match, you will see regular changes in fielding positions as the captain tries to outwit the batsmen in an effort to get a result.

The captain is a much respected man, and his skills decide how much respect he earns. If you should ever be offered the captaincy of your team, accept it only if you have the confidence to do the job well and if you honestly feel you can earn the respect of your team mates.

Ex-England skipper Geoffrey Boycott (Yorkshire) playing one of the many strokes that he was master at, the square-drive. Note how Boycott is not wearing a protective helmet: they only started becoming more widely used in his latter days as a first-class player.

USEFUL ADDRESSES

Australian Cricket Board
70, Jolimont Street
Jolimont
Victoria
3002
Australia

Board of Control for Cricket in India
Vijay Nagar Colony
Bhiwani 125 021
India

Board of Control for Cricket in Pakistan
Gadaffi Stadium
Lahore
Pakistan

Board of Control for Cricket in Sri Lanka
35 Maitland Place
Colombo 7
Sri Lanka

Club Cricket Conference
353 West Barnes Lane
New Malden
Surrey
KT3 6JF

Cricket Council
Lord's Ground
London
NW8 8QN

International Cricket Conference
Lord's Ground
London
NW8 8QN

Marylebone Cricket Club
Lord's Ground
London
NW8 8QN

Minor Counties Cricket Association
Thorpe Cottage
Mill Common
Ridlington
North Walsham
NR28 9TY

National Cricket Association
Lord's Ground
London
NW8 8QN

USEFUL · ADDRESSES

New Zealand Cricket Council
PO Box 958
Christchurch
New Zealand

West Indies Cricket Board of Control
8B Caledonia Avenue
Kingston 5
Jamaica

Women's Cricket Association
16 Upper Woburn Place
London
WC1 0QP

RULES CLINIC
INDEX

**The perfect action of the fast bowler, Joel Garner of the West
Indies. Note the 'unused' arm pointing towards the target and the
bowler's eyes fixed on the area he intends pitching to.**

INDEX

Figures in *italics* indicate illustrations.